NOW
WHA

Ur
Myths

NOW! THAT'S WHAT I CALL

Urban Myths

Phil Healey & Rick Glanvill

First published in Great Britain in 1996 by
Virgin Books
an imprint of Virgin Publishing Ltd
332 Ladbroke Grove
LONDON W10 5AH

A catalogue record for this book is available from the
British Library.

ISBN 0 86369 969 3

Phototypeset by Intype London Ltd

Printed and bound in Great Britain by
Mackays of Chatham PLC, Chatham, Kent

contents

package; Wrong ring; Charge of the light brigade; Mexican waves; Cow down below!; State of shock; Caught in the headlights; Hidden extras; Motorway deliverance; Pull the other one; Quite a climax; Wash day blues; The appliance of science; The driving dog; Hitched up; A nasty set-to; Mythellaneous

the long *arm of the law*
Scams and scamsters
63

Fat filly foils felony; Backwards in the fast lane; Blue light spells danger; 'This is a pick-up!'; Signed, sealed and delivered; Crisp business; Foul play; Take the tube; An unfair cop; Blue murder; Radio daze; Court out; Motorway madness; A dead halt; Crimebotch UK; Mythellaneous

food *and drink*
Half-baked hiccups
79

The office party and Mr Byrite; The sickly city slicker; The night stalker; Chinese poodle; Southern-fried rodent; An offal experience; Nowt taken out; Keep it under your hat; Peanut; Fruity salad; One lump or two?; You must be choking; Gums and plums; A sour note; The prime cut; Slap happy; The fist anniversary; Bottoms up; Mythellaneous

man's *best friends*
A menagerie of animal crackers
97

Taking the mickey; The dead rabbit; Sex with Nanny; Monkey-hanging business; Paws for thought; Uncool for cats; Yucky Yucca; Dirty dog; Bacon lined; Posing pouch; The dead budgie; Horse shoot; Messy moggy; Ruff guide to Spain; Cat in the bag; Feather light; Walkies!; Horse play; The labrador let-off; Underhand undercarriage; Red or dead; Cat eats dog; Dummy hunt; Dressing for dinner; Caught shortly; Mythellaneous

occupational *hazards*
Nine-to-five nonsense
127

The deer-stalker; Papier man-mâché; The carpet creeper; Plumbing new depths; Incoming tax; Super fly guy; A miner tiff; Playing away; Highly unrealistic; Trouble brewing; Broom with a view; So re-spectable; The cavity cowboys; Making a splash; Supply and demand; Punch lines; Shelf-help scheme; Badly stiched up; Going overboard; Last for Best; Quite Frankly; The bottle of Britain; Mythellaneous

wish *you were here?*
Trouble abroad
153

The ring of confidence; Odd customs; Don't fetch!: Out of the fishing boat, into the fire; The naked ski-girl; Rollerballs; Welcome to Dallas; The kidney burglar; The Empire

State escape; 'Hit the deck, lady'; The buggering Bronx Batman; The Mexican tobacco pouch; Walt's and all; Measure for measure; The taste of Greece; Midnight run; Underground service; Double your money; Wang end of the stick; Dolomite triumph; Taken for a ride; Turned out nasty again; Bombay cow; Mythellaneous

surgical *spirit*
Medicine balls
179

Gone to seed; Four eyes only; The hair nest; The back eye; Sticky situation; Wagging it; Pea soup; From beer to eternity; As directed; Getting the point; Body and soul; Tijuana flu; Just earsay; Finger-licking good; Mythellaneous

x-rated
On-the-job jams
195

Kinky K.O.; Lovers' lock; A sad reflection; Chicken gobble; Fit for nothing; Tits first; Revenge is . . . ; The botty bottle; Bangkok Bill; More cake, vicar?; The party pooper; Below the belt; Mr and Mrs; Mr Blobby on the job; Rub-a-dub; The genital touch; Her pedigree chum; The bus seductress; Balls bounced; Massage virgin; Lady luck; Hamming it up; Beeb boob; Corporal punishment; The bishop's wife; Trouser snake'n'vac; Behind with the milk; A relative shock; Express your love; Nec-romancer; Mythellaneous

friends *and relations*

Nowt so queer as folk

Atlantic potion; A fart amongst friends; That sinking feeling; The old man and the teeth; Down the hatch; Go ferret; Phone home; Naïvety play; Passing out; A friend of the family; Home and away; A smashing honeymoon; Five-year hitch; Take a chance; Privatised depression; Paperboy; Pole-axed; Robin red-face; Golf war; Going, going, totally gone . . . ; Dead cert; A queer reason; Left baggage; The Xmas family break-in; Shedding a load; House of horrors; Mythellaneous

wan*ted*

acknow*ledgements*

Phil Healey and Rick Glanvill would like to thank the following people for their contribution to the success of the *Urban Myths* series:

Tony Ageh, Robin Allen, Mick Armson, Sarah Ball, Albert Becker, David Bonney, John Boyd, Penny Brunton, Andy Brice, Bill Broadhead, Billy Budd, Martin 'Woosie' Bullock, Roy Carr, Gez and Penny Casey, Ian Cassidy, Clare the printer, Yael, Yona and Miriam Cohen, Steve Collier, Paul 'Big Ears' 'Blabbermouth' 'Juggler' 'Crojo' Crome, J. Glyn Davies, Andrew Denny, Diane Taylor, Julie Douglas, Big John Eichler, D. Fleetwood, Andy Forbes-Gower, Paul Gallagher, Bobbie, Johnny, Gary and Sarah Glanvill, Steve Glennon, Bobby Greenland, Richard Greenleaf, Peter Hanington, Stephen Harris, John and Sarah Hartwell, Dave Heywood, Irene, Ray and Nigel Healey, Graham Hopwood, David Hurran, Ian Hutchings, Joe at the *Guardian*, Joe from Lagos, Scott and Mary Johnston, Robin Ely Jones, Stuart Jones, Brendan Joyce, Jamie Keenan, Dave Kimberley, Debbie King, Frances Lloyd, Emma Loveridge, John 'Squaddie' Ludlam, Michael Patrick Aloysius McCoy, David McDonald, Dave Martin, Sara Miller, Chris Morris, Richard Newton, David Newstead, Al Nicholls, Chris Padmore, Dave Percival, Al and Ceri Preston, Mike Rayner, Colin Richards, Dave 'the Avenger' and Jessica Rigg, Lindsay Roberts, James Roff, Kathy Rooney, 'Barney' McCarthy, Steve Rumney, Jonathon A. Salt, John Sandford, Paul Screeton, Satwinder 'Turban Myths' Sehmi, John 'Skins' Skinner, Willie Smax, Sue Smallwood, Smiffy and Co.,

A. H. Smith, Peter Spanton, Alex Stainsby, Hilary Steele, Brett Stevens, Wg Cmdr Alex Stewart, Roy Stringer, Mick Suett, Dave Talbot, Chris Tarrant, Robert Urbanus, Mark 'Urgent' Urgent, Martin Vallis, Nigel Vernon, Carol Wilhide, Selma Wong, Chippy Wood, Tim Woolgar and Wouter Van Zijc.

A general showbiz-type thank you to Katie Davies, Les Newman, Christine Williams, Judy Finnegan and Richard Madeley and the thousands of callers into *This Morning* (a lovely programme), Nick Knowles from *Coast to Coast*, that bloke who sat next to us on *TV-AM* while we plugged the second book (Mike something or other), those people who jammed the switchboard during Shyama Pereira's show on GLR, LBC's Derek Hobson and the Robbie Vincent Show, Danny Baker for his indecent exposure of our books on Radio 5, the various radio presenters on all the stations across Britain, Malcolm Elliot, Ranald McDonald and Brian Bury in Oz, Deborah Orr at the *Guardian*, Radio 1's top Marks, Radcliffe and Riley (Lard), Liz Kershaw, Steve Wright, Ian Hislop and *Private Eye*, and the researchers at *Good Morning with Anne and Nick*.

Cheers to: Tony Ageh, Mervyn Ashford, Sarah Ball, Paul Baker, Albert Becker, Alan Bird, Alan Broadhead, 'Nicolai Ceausescu', Tony Collingwood, Julie Douglas, Keith Drummond, Deke and John Eichler, Phil Eccles, Danny Flynn, Emma Freud, Andy Horn, Mark Lawson, Ken Livingstone, Alex MacLean, Ian McCarthy, Kwesi Mansah, Andy Medlock, Jan O'Neil, Q, Mick Quirke, Monique Roffey, Richard Schram, Willy Smax, Jessica Stevens, Jill Thompson, Mark Webster, Tim Woolgar and Steve Wright.

And to: Dr D. A. Pantony, Dr Jon Hobman, Dr H. B.

Chipengwa, Adam Curtin, Iona at Acid Jazz, Annabel at MTV, Matt Preston, Stan Crowther, K. D. McBride, Steve Avery, Sandra Hyman, John Hunter, Chris Bewis, Phil Shaw, Steve Glennon, Nathan Collins, Frosula Taliadorou, Paul Patterson, Erica Caithness, Stuart Kirkham, Big Matt from Burnley, Gerry Clarke, Caroline Boucher, God the creator, M. B. Hudson, Bob Smythe, Tim Woolgar, Deirdre Mason, David Powell, Zoe James, Jim Judges, Jen Cox, David Bonney, Sean from Windsor, Matthew from St Albans, Terry the cabbie, Aubrey from Barnes, David from Guildford, John from Chingford, Eileen Bethell, David Mitchell, Venetia out there in Claygate, Andrew Gibson, George Wray, Carlos Sapochnik, Frank Desmond, Jeff Gamble, Andy Giles, Bryan Simpson, Neal Cooper, Mrs Robinson, Mike Campbell.

Thanks also to anyone else we've forgotten to mention, to our agent Cat Ledger and the staff at Virgin Publishing, and to those excellent hostelries, The Hope in Smithfield and The Three Kings in Clerkenwell.

intro*duction*

What you now hold in your hands (with certain reservations, especially if you're in the bath) is the product of years, nay centuries, of evolution and hard graft – not, we hasten to add, all on our part.

Popular myths have dogged civilisation's footsteps throughout the ascent of man. The modern 'urban' variety comprise fascinating, funny or occasionally horrific stories that are told as true but have highly dubious origins. They usually happen to a friend of a friend, or other vague acquaintance.

The stories are usually too good to be true, involve far too many convenient coincidences and the endings are often beyond belief.

Like jokes, apocryphal tales act as a release valve for twentieth-century obsessions, bigotries and fears. And they are tales from the paranoid metropolis unlike their older, folksier rustic cousins. Hence 'urban' myths.

When, in the winter of '91, we first sat down with the intention of uncovering as many urban myths as possible for publication, we had high hopes for a grand collection. Several weeks – and pints – later, we had about fifteen (printable). But boy, were they good ones!

Happily, Virgin Publishing saw this as no impediment, and we have subsequently provided them, thus far, with three collections. Our painstaking research, plus the overwhelming response from family, friends, acquaintances, readers, phone-in callers and many others, has meant that we have now published around 1,000 of the most frequently told examples of popular mythology, taking the folklore world by storm.

We are eternally grateful to the hundreds of myth-lovers from around the world who contributed in so many ways to the huge success of the first three books – *Urban Myths*, *The Return of Urban Myths*, and *Urban Myths Unplugged* – but we shall still expect them to dig deep and shell out for this 'best of'.

We would also like to express our gratitude once again to those who helped spread the message on TV, radio and in print. How could we forget those cheery smiles, all the wonderful, funny, fascinating people . . . and Jim Davidson.

Healey & Glanvill

urban *classics*

The cream of the crop

Blow the dust off these cherished old classics, as we parade our well-worn chestnuts for inspection. These hoary old collectables have been handed down from generation to generation, and readers won't need the *Antiques Roadshow* to tell them some of these heirlooms have been around since the Magna Carta. Add this treasure trove of fascinating pieces, honed by time, to your collection. They don't make 'em like this any more, madam.

the hairy *hand*

Late one night, my uncle's old school mate was driving home from Whitechapel to Barking. At the time, there had been a number of savage attacks on women waiting for late-night buses, and this was, of course, the old stalking ground of Jack The Ripper. It was dark, foul weather – windy, and really bucketing it down – and as he was driving through Stepney, he saw a woman crouched under a bus stop. With the thought of this attacker around, he decided to stop and give her a lift at least some part of her journey. So he pulled up and the drenched figure got in. He began trying to make conversation with his passenger, who he noted was well built and didn't know how to apply make-up properly, but to no avail.

Several attempts having led to nothing but a grunt, the driver took a sneaky closer look, and noticed to his consternation that the hands clutched round the handbag were extremely hairy and muscular. The more he looked at the person next to him, the more he panicked.

He decided on a plan. 'Could you just nip out quickly and check my back lights?' he asked, 'because that car just flashed me and I think they might not be working.' The shady figure obliged. The driver slammed the door shut, rammed the accelerator to the floor and sped to the nearest police station. As he screeched to a halt outside, he noticed that the 'woman' had left the handbag in the front, so he presented it for inspection when he nervously burbled his story.

'Looks like you've had a lucky escape, sir,' said the duty sergeant, producing from the bag a shiny, blood-stained hatchet.

One of the author's uncles related this yarn over ten years ago, and still maintains it happened exactly like that. When it was pointed out that similar stories of hirsute, axe-wielding t.v.s have circulated all over UK cities for years (notably Chapeltown in Leeds during the time of the Yorkshire Ripper), he gave us an old-fashioned look.

the fingered *felon*

This Glasgow couple I heard about went out for the evening. When they got back in the house later, they were greeted by their pit-bull terrier, but he seemed more subdued than usual. Then he started choking and wretching, so they patted him increasingly hard on the back, but to no avail. They looked up an emergency vet and rushed him round there.

The vet opened the pit-bull's mouth and looked in, then said he could see something blocking its throat. Because the dog was so vicious, he put him under sedation before removing the obstruction. It turned out to be two bloody human fingers.

'I should ring the police,' said the vet, handing them the phone.

The couple rushed home to meet the police, who set about searching the house. In an upstairs bedroom, there was a trail of blood leading to a wardrobe. Inside cowered a would-be burglar clutching his mutilated hand, and unconscious from loss of blood.

the poodle in *the microwave*

A rich elderly lady from Harrogate was taking her pet poodle out for a walk when they were caught in a downpour. Rushing back inside, fretful for her pampered pet, she was desperate to dry him out and warm him up as soon as possible. So she took him straight into the kitchen, opened the door of her daughter's new microwave cooker for the first time, and thrust him in, moving the dial to a moderate setting. She patted his head and carefully closed the door with a click.

The old lady was still drying her hair when the cooked dog exploded, ripping the door off the microwave.

A popular 'tabloids' story, this one. Some people tell the 12" extended play version which suggests that the woman placed the hapless dog in the microwave because she'd become used to putting it in her old electric cooker for a minute or two to warm up when this sort of drenching had occurred in the past – an echo of the other story about the babysitters putting the little one's head in the gas oven for a minute to slip it back into the land of nod. It's also sometimes mischievously added that the woman sued the manufacturer of the hi-tech appliance over the incident . . . and won her case, because it didn't say anywhere in the instructions that you shouldn't dry off your poodle inside the contraption.

the vanishing *hitchhiker*

A friend of a friend was cruising down the A1 to London when he passed a young lady standing by the side of the road. He pulled up and asked her if she needed a lift. Without speaking, she got into the car. He was quite attracted to her, so he tried to get her talking, but she just wouldn't say anything, not even where she was getting off. Instead, at the junction, she pointed. Then at her road, and then at her house, where she got out of the car. He drove off in a huff.

A couple of days later, he was looking for something in the car when he came across a woman's coat. Knowing it must be the hitchhiker's, he retraced his route to return the coat to her. So he knocked on the door and an older lady opened it. He held out the coat and explained that he wanted to return it to the young woman. The woman burst into tears. 'Yes, it was my daughter's,' she spluttered, 'but she was killed on the A1 five years ago.'

the *hook*

Many years back, a young couple were canoodling in a lovers' lane on the edge of town. The radio was playing and the car was well steamed up. The lovers' clinch was broken when a stern voice interrupted the light programme and announced that a local criminal asylum had reported a breakout and that there was a homicidal maniac on the prowl. The man was extremely dangerous and should on no account be approached. He was easily identifiable, it said, as he had a very distinguishing feature – a hook instead of a hand on one arm.

The announcement sent a shiver down the girl's spine and thoroughly put the dampers on her ardour. She insisted on being driven home immediately. Chronically dischuffed, the boyfriend started the car and sped off back to her parents' at a rate of knots. When they got back, the boyfriend, ever the gent, went round to open her door, and was horrified to find a steely hook dangling from the handle.

the man in *the back*

A Cardiff woman was driving home alone one dark night, and came up to a slip road on to the M5. There wasn't that much traffic, so she was putting her foot down a bit. But as she got on to the motorway, she looked ahead of her and was alarmed to see what looked like a little child lying down by the hard shoulder. She screeched to a halt and immediately ran to see if she could help.

When she got closer, though, she saw that it was just a big, lifelike doll. She was relieved and returned to her car, but as she did, a dark car, going quite slowly, cruised up behind hers, flashing its headlamps at her. Not a little concerned that this might turn nasty, she decided to hurry home a.s.a.p.

But as she roared off, the car stuck close to her, following her every detour and flashing again and again. She then realised this was a pretty threatening situation, and as there was no-one at her home, headed instead for her friend's house. The car was now trying to overtake her, and there was a shadowy figure in the driving seat waving his hands around aggressively.

Finally, she swerved to a halt by her friend's house and

ran out. The bloke in the other car dashed out, ran up to her and said, 'Wait! I was trying to warn you! When you stopped before, someone got in the back of your car.' They both looked round, to see a thin, raggedy man scampering away down the road.

the secretary's *sexy surprise*

A middle-aged boss was feeling the years slipping away from him and sensed his frisky days might be numbered, and was trying his best to forget his birthday again – the big 5-0. His family seemed to be doing likewise. There was no mention of his special day at breakfast, and his wife even said that she was going to the theatre that night. He imagined he might spend his birthday alone in front of the telly. So when his charming young secretary suggested they might go out for a drink after work, he jumped at the idea (and hoped for another jump later). The two had a nice evening, and with each cocktail he was getting hotter for her. Eventually she suggested she drive him back to his place. When they arrived there, he put his arm around her and implored her to come in for a coffee – it was still quite early.

Once inside, the secretary ran ahead of him, turned out the lights and led him into the living-room and told him to stay there while she 'fixed up a special birthday treat for him'. Imagining that the nature of this treat was sexual, the boss began hurriedly to remove all this clothes.

Minutes later, as he stood in naked, fumbling anticipation of what was about to happen, all the lights suddenly went on, and he was confronted by all his family, friends and workmates shouting 'Surprise!!'

Another version of this well-worn tale involves a couple coming back from a romantic meal for two celebrating their wedding anniversary, who feel a bit fruity, go into the front room and strip off. They are caught naked, *in flagrante delicto*, when their friends burst in with the traditional 'Surprise!!'

the turkey *trot*

A friend of a friend bought his Christmas turkey from a local farm last year, determined to have a full-flavoured dish for the big day.

He loved his Christmas dinner, it was the culinary high-spot of his year, with golden roast turkey, roast potatoes, sprouts, stuffing and floods of gravy – smashing.

The bloke picked up the heavy, pre-plucked fowl on Christmas Eve. It was so fresh it still felt warm. He bundled the dead weight into his car, drove home feeling especially festive, and squeezed the huge roaster into his fridge as soon as he got in.

The next morning, he woke up especially early to gut and season the big bird. When he opened the fridge door, however, he had something of a surprise.

Apparently the huge bald gobbler had only been stunned by the farmer.

Furious at its frosty captivity and sore at the plucking, it lunged out of the fridge and savaged the hapless bloke, before smashing through the French windows to freedom.

an 'L' of an accident

A friend of a friend was taking his motorcycle driving test a few years ago on a local estate of back-to-back terraced houses. It was a grey and drizzly day, and all the dreary streets looked the same.

The test itself involved the learner riding around an agreed circuit. At certain points the stony-faced examiner would be watching, checking certain manoeuvres and ticking things off against his list.

The learner was pretty nervous, but the test seemed to be trundling along quite well. Then the examiner flagged him down and said he was about to test his emergency stop.

He told the biker to continue driving around the streets and at some point he would jump out and shout 'Stop!'

All tensed up, the biker set off round the streets. A few minutes later he'd completed most of the circuit and the examiner still hadn't jumped out.

Then, when he rounded the last corner, he saw an agitated group of people in the middle of the road. They were gathered round the pole-axed, out-cold examiner.

Apparently he'd 'tested' the wrong bike.

> That one's been around since the introduction of the bike test soon after the Second World War and really doesn't seem to have altered. Even in today's sophisticated society people seem to get a kick out of authority coming a cropper.

a lousy *night out*

For her hen-night treat, a friend of a friend went with some mates to see one of those raunchy male stripper acts.

The ladies were having a riot ogling the hunky fellas' bulging pecs. They were all getting over-excited, shrieking as the gyrating Adonises disrobed.

Apparently, the bride-to-be got a little tipsy and forced her way to the front of the stage to get a better view. Dancing in a frenzy, she was almost overcome when, at the climax of his act, one of the writhing oiled hunks whipped off his shiny G-string and flung it on to her face.

A couple of days later she was checking her complexion in the bathroom mirror when she noticed a spot near her eyelid. This blemish was a little worrying; with the wedding at the weekend she wanted to look her best for the photographs.

Over the next few days, she tried every kind of cream, but the spot just got larger and larger until she was driven to visit the doctor.

The quack took one look, and informed the girl that he'd have to operate immediately: she had a pubic louse living in her face.

> Our publishers told us on no account to mention the Chippendales anywhere near that story, so we won't. Even so, this myth has rapidly done the rounds since the disrobing hunks arrived on the scene – there must be a lot of disgruntled boyfriends eagerly passing it on.

a shocking *blunder*

A friend of a friend had been outdoors on his patch preparing for his favourite time of year, blooming spring.

It had rained persistently for days before, so the green-fingered enthusiast ensured he put on his wellington boots before he went out weeding.

After a few hours tugging, he'd done as much as he could handle, wheeled his trusty barrow into the garden shed and walked a little wearily round to the front of the house into the garage, where he'd left his other shoes.

He lifted the up-and-over door, then turned on the light, leaning next to the switch while employing the time-honoured welly-removing technique of putting one foot on the heel of the other boot and pushing.

In his tiredness the bloke was struggling with the troublesome footwear: wobbling about, tugging on the stuck gumboot and almost losing his footing.

Apparently, a nosy neighbour, washing his car across the road, spotted the jerking gardener with his hand on the light switch, and put two and two together.

The good Samaritan leapt across the road, picking up a handy baseball bat and aiming to break the hapless gardener's contact with the switch and save him from electrocution.

In a frenzy of misplaced goodwill, he whacked the bat down as hard as possible, breaking his bewildered neighbour's arm in two places.

> Another tale that's really going places at the moment, and of which there are two interesting variations: in one the action takes place on an allotment and the injured party leans on a pylon to take his boots off (his father whacks him with a spade to break the contact); and in the other the setting is a kitchen, where a jerking young man is seen holding a wire with his hand on the electric kettle – his wife hits him with a rolling pin to stop the electrocution, but he was only dancing along to the music on his personal stereo.

hard *to swallow*

A friend of a friend was enjoying the holiday of a lifetime exploring the Amazon rainforest.

She'd been warned about the perilous nature of the local

12

fauna, and not to swim in the river itself no matter how dirty and hot she got.

Apparently the temptation proved too much, and she decided to risk a refreshing naked immersion in the tropical Amazonian water. She was having a wonderful time practising her breaststroke, until her chin dipped under the surface and she swallowed something that made her choke. She was forced to retire to the bank to recover her composure.

After a while back in Britain, the woman found she was acquiring a voracious appetite for food. Yet her bingeing was having no effect on her waif-like waist.

Soon she was insatiable, tucking into absolutely anything edible. But, incredibly, she was *losing* weight, and her stomach still ached with hunger.

Naturally concerned, she consulted her doctor, who felt her stomach and suggested a prompt visit to a hospital casualty.

They operated at once, and opened up her intestines. There they found a pale, eight-foot anaconda that had grown inside her from the egg she'd inadvertently swallowed.

it's a *lick-up*

A young woman known to a friend in the pub used to live in a spooky old house with her parents in Bath.

When she was sixteen, she was bought a playful puppy which she absolutely adored and which returned her affection twice over. The little spaniel was particularly comforting when her parents stayed away for the night and she was left alone in the rambling, ancient house.

On one such occasion, a nasty windswept night, the

teenager played with her puppy before going to sleep, and allowed the dog to sleep on her bed for companionship.

Halfway through the night, she was woken by a tickling sensation on her foot. She clumsily reached under the duvet to push her affectionate puppy away, but he'd already gone.

A little later the same thing happened. Still half asleep, she again shooed the playful mutt away. A few hours passed and the puppy started licking again. But this time after she'd moved her foot away, she became aware of an annoying dripping sound in the bathroom. She wasn't going to get up just to turn a tap off, so she put her head down and didn't wake again until morning.

When she got up, her puppy was nowhere to be seen, but the dripping was still going on, much slower now, so she went straight to the bathroom. To her horror, there in the bathroom was her poor, bloodied puppy, hanging up over the sink with its throat cut. And chillingly daubed on the mirror in canine blood was the legend 'Humans can lick too.'

upstairs, *downstairs*

There was a babysitter working for a well-off family I knew in Sheffield who one evening received some disturbing phone calls. At first they were just heavy breathing, but when the caller began to threaten murder and made it clear he knew where she was, the babysitter rang the police. It was a huge house and quite spooky anyway.

The police were very good, and told her they'd immediately put a trace on the calls, and to keep the bloke talking next time. A little later, the phone rang again. It was the same caller, so she strung him along as much as she could, even though he was saying the most blood-curdling and offensive things to her. Eventually he hung up. But the phone rang again straight away. It was the police.

'Get out of there immediately!' shouted an officer. 'We traced the call, and it was the other phone line at your house. The nutter's upstairs!'

> Variations on this theme have been the stuff of shoestring budget horror movies for decades. Sometimes, as in the Audrey Hepburn movie *After Dark*, the threatened woman is blind, or the caller is the policeman himself.

roll out the *dead carpet*

There was a family from Surrey who decided to spend their vacation in France, taking their elderly grandma with them. Granny spent all their stay complaining. Well, not quite all of it, because a little way into the holiday, she died on them.

Deciding that the old woman would hate not to be buried in her beloved Blighty, the family set about returning her home, and, mindful of the customs and other problems they might face, they resolved to hide her. So they bought a cheap bit of carpet, and rolled the wrinkled little corpse up in it. Granny's body was by now too stiff to bend on to a car seat, so they had to strap her on the roof-rack. In this way she was driven across France for two days, through driving rain and baking sunshine, across the Channel by ferry, and finally all the way home.

Unhappily, having made it back without a hitch, the family were devastated when, after a well-earned cuppa, they went outside to find the car had been stolen – carpet, Granny and all. And they were never recovered.

> We've heard of numerous international versions
> of this classic dilemma. In the States, the trip is
> to Mexico, and in Spain, it's to Portugal . . .

the memory *man*

The brother of the secretary of our local philately society went on holiday to America in the 1980s and hit the heritage trail as soon as he arrived: Wild West ghost towns, War of Independence landmarks, Japanese car manufacturers . . . the lot.

One day the tour guide directed his charges to a native American reservation, where he recommended that the Limey visitors check out the legendary local 'memory man', a grey, gnarled old American Indian who made Keith Richards look like Tom Cruise. He could remember the most incredible everyday detail from the last sixty years, the guide assured them.

Having crossed the old cove's palm with the requisite silver, the tourist then posed the single question he was permitted to ask: 'What did you have for breakfast twenty-five years ago today?' he queried. 'Two eggs,' said the old chief, enigmatically. With no way to disprove this, the Brit withdrew, not particularly impressed.

Eight years later, on another jaunt across the Americas, the same tourist found himself driving through familiar territory – he was near the reservation with the amazing antique recollector. 'Ah hah,' he thought, 'Let's see how good his memory really is – I wonder if he'll remember *me*.'

Making his way to the old moth-eaten teepee, the visitor slipped inside and sat down unannounced opposite the ancient sage. Then he greeted him as he saw fit, beginning, 'How!'

'Scrambled,' muttered the old man, sucking serenely on his pipe.

the surgical *clipper*

During the heyday of punk rock in Devon – 1982 – a friend of a friend was working as a porter in a general hospital. Apart from a litany of unusual foreign bodies found in patients' various orifices, his favourite story concerned a punk rocker admitted one day for treatment for a broken thigh bone.

The snarling waif had safety pins through every protuberance, moribund-style make-up and a startling shock of green hair. When she was put under anaesthetic and disrobed for the bone-pinning and leg-plastering operation, the surgeon was not altogether surprised to see that the punky patient's pubic hair was dyed green too, and above it was tattooed the saucy legend: 'KEEP OFF THE GRASS.' Naturally, for hygiene reasons, this had to be removed, and was swiftly shaved off.

An hour later, operation satisfactorily completed, the young woman was returned to her ward, where she shortly regained consciousness. Studying the full-leg plaster for the first time, she was embarrassed to read the surgeon's ironic felt-tipped message: 'SORRY, I'M AFRAID WE HAD TO MOW THE LAWN.'

travel *bug*

A woman well-known to our family friends was the travelling type, always hopping off to exotic places. One year, she set her heart on Guatemala in Central America. She went with an adventure holiday tour, which took people into the wild interior – lots of hacking through jungle with a machete and bivouacking overnight amidst the sounds of the rainforest. The woman was game and loved roughing it, so she wasn't at all fazed by all the creepie-crawlies everywhere, and had one of the best holidays she could remember.

When she returned home to England, she noticed that a bite on her cheek she had sustained early on in the jungle had not healed up and was beginning to itch. She put some cream on it and thought no more about it.

After a few days, however, the swelling had grown very bad indeed, and soon, despite applying various creams, the woman looked in the mirror and saw the whole cheek was red, itchy and inflamed. Finally, finding the irritation too much, the woman gave her cheek a really good scratch. At which the skin cracked, and hundreds of tiny spiders burst out, scattering away across her face.

> Which all goes to show: never trust Incy-Wincy, the unpredictable little arachnid with anti-personnel habits. Paradoxically, in classic Caribbean myth, 'Anansi the spider' is a resourceful hero to be admired and emulated.

highway *to heaven*

An alderman from Tadcaster in Yorkshire, where all the best beer comes from (apart from Boddingtons and Courage, of course), knew a local parson who had encountered his fair share of adversity. Once the venerable old cleric was driving his brand new Austin Seven (we're talking about a while ago) through the summery dales when it spluttered and conked out.

The padre was distraught. He had a wedding to officiate in an hour. It was at the next village some miles away and now he'd foolishly run out of petrol. Then remembering that he'd passed a garage a short while back he clasped his hands together, praised the Lord and, gathering his cassock about him, set off at a pace.

Upon reaching the garage he enquired of the pump attendant whether there was a receptacle into which he might put a gallon or so to alleviate his predicament. The grease monkey shook his head glumly, then pointed to a scrap heap out the back and burbled, 'Mebbes yowl fand summat over yon, reverun'.'

The vicar scrambled about on the rubbish tip, but the only thing he could lay his hands on was a child's enamel potty. There was nothing else for it. He'd have to use that, unsuited to the task though it was. Filling the gusunder (goes under the baby, gedditt?) to the brim, he set off back to his stranded motor.

It was the middle of summer and the vicar began to build up quite a sweat, especially when he realised that the yellowy liquid was rapidly evaporating from his open receptacle. He reached the car with but a dribble left and was just pouring the dregs into the petrol tank when a

19

gleaming Bentley purred up. A dowager in the back, all wrapped up in mink, saw the red-faced clergyman at his task.

'Oh parson,' she sighed, 'I wish I had your faith.'

dober*manned*

A smashing couple called Teh and Caz moved on to a new estate in one of Liverpool's outlying districts and immediately caused concern among the rest of the Toxteth farmers (Scousers who'd moved into the sticks to better themselves with a bit of garden). The reason for this was not their manner or anything they did, but the fact they brought with them their two adored and slavering hounds – vicious identical twin Dobermans – that were forever running through an oversize cat flap into the garden and irritating neighbours with their noisy, brutal playing.

But the owners soon settled in the area, and made many new friends. In particular, they hit it off with their next-door neighbour, and when after nearly a year in residence they asked if he would look after their dogs while they were away for a week, the neighbour readily agreed, despite his fear of the pets.

The first few days were uneventful. The neighbour put the dogs' food in a bowl and poked it through a gap under the garden fence, and both dogs would rush out through the cat flap to scoff it, greedily nuzzling each other out of the way.

But after three days, the helpful neighbour noticed something strange: when he pushed the edibles under the fence, only one of the sneering beasts came through the hatch. The next day, the same thing happened: just one of the deranged beasts emerged. The bloke began to wonder if the hound had bumped off its twin, or whether it was simply ill. A few days later, although he was terrified, the neighbour girded his loins and decided to investigate. He couldn't stand letting his new friends down.

So he gingerly climbed over the fence brandishing the door keys, and let himself into the house. The dogs were evidently upstairs, judging by the sound of their growling and sneering. Sneaking up the stairs so as not to provoke the dogs, the neighbour looked over the banister on the landing and was shocked at the scene in the bedroom.

For three days the two Dobermans, their faces screwed up in a hellish sneer, had apparently been terrorising a young would-be burglar, now a quivering wreck covered in blood and far from hygienic in the toilet department. The mad mutts had been working in shifts, taking it in turns to eat and then keep the burglar at bay.

> It's usually added that the intruder was so psycho-
> logically disturbed by his experience that he was
> never fit enough to stand trial.

the *goat*

Some friends were on an angling holiday in north Cornwall, sea-fishing off the cliffs. The fish were refusing to bite, and not much was happening generally, until one of the blokes went wandering and discovered an abandoned stone well half-buried among some bushes.

They decided to see how deep it was by dropping a small pebble into the shaft. The stone whistled down the echoey chasm and eventually splashed quietly at the bottom. So they threw a bigger rock down, then an even bigger one. It was much more fun than fishing.

Eventually one of the blokes found a large steel spike and threw that down. As he did, there was a sudden rustling in the shrubbery.

The lads noticed the bar was attached to a long chain, which began to rattle through the grass, gathering momentum, until suddenly a tethered goat burst through the bushes, was dragged past them bleating frantically, and hurtled down the well.

> Other settings for this billy goat gaffe you may have come across include ski resorts near deep crevasses, the Lake District with its deep potholes, and rocky parts of Spain.

welcome to *Butlin's*

An acquaintance from Lancashire was enjoying her well-earned summer holiday, with smiling hubby at the wheel of the family Ford Zodiac cutting a swathe down to Clacton. The kids had only said 'Are we there yet?' a dozen or so times, the sun was shining and they had a fortnight in Butlin's to look forward to – what could be better? The journey had been a breeze and as they cruised towards the thronging camp with its inviting neon sign their hearts leapt.

It was perfect, everything a Wake's Week family could dream of: fairground, hairdressers, full English fry-up, late-night chippy, talent nights and cheap beer on-site and on tap. The moment they arrived a jolly Redcoat led them past row after row of happy holiday homes to their bijou prefab chalet with all mod cons; there was even a shower and bunk beds for the kids.

The chatty Redcoat handed over the key with a cheery wave and the kids pelted off to the amusements. At last the parents were alone.

'I'm off to use that shower to wash away the grime of that long drive,' the husband crooned, stepping out of his trousers with a saucy wink. 'Come and join me if you like . . .'

'I'll just pop out and get some provisions from that little shop we passed,' replied the wife. And she danced out of the door, swinging her shopping bag like a satchel.

A few minutes later, her carrier bulging, she skipped in through the open chalet door. Spotting her naked spouse towelling himself dry with his back to her, she lunged forward, grasped his wedding tackle and bellowed 'Welcome to Butlin's!' while nibbling his ear.

The bloke nearly died of fright – she'd got the wrong chalet and goosed a complete stranger.

> When that one appeared in our regular column in the Weekend section of the Saturday *Guardian*, we received an interesting correspondence from Mr Stan Crowther which gives us a clue about the nature of 'mythologising'. Pleased to see his work established in the nation's folklore, he suggests that the Butlin's story derives from a folk song he wrote and performed over thirty years ago, called A Visit To Butlin's. From which, we hereby reproduce the final, cautionary verse:

'So come all married women, take a warning by
me –
If you go off to Butlin's for a week by the sea,
Be sure you can recognise the man you have wed
Even when his shirt's right over his head.'

Excellent stuff.

the chamber *pot*

A mate from college got friendly with a rich kid and was
invited to a party at the latter's 'country retreat'. He
accepted and was looking forward to a glimpse of how the
other half lives.

The house was amazing – a real mansion – absolutely
massive and in enormous grounds. My mate felt well out
of his depth, but really enjoyed himself and got so drunk
he virtually had to be carried to his room on the second
floor.

He woke up in the middle of the night needing to relieve
himself, and with a wicked headache. He knew there was
a chamber pot under the bed, because he'd had a good
laugh at it when he arrived, but he wanted to do number
twos and it would've been embarrassing to do it in a pot.
So he left his room and set off to find the toilet in the
house's labyrinths. He looked all along the corridor, but
every door had a snoring occupant behind it, so he gave
up and resolved to use the chamber pot after all. Much
relieved, he drifted back to sleep.

In the morning he was awoken by a bell and cries to
come down for breakfast, but he needed to have a leak

first, which he did, and then decided that, sober, he'd easily find a toilet where he could flush away the pot's contents.

Leaving the offending porcelain behind, he looked along the corridor and again couldn't locate the WC. Giving up on it, and still a little tipsy, he thought he might as well throw the stuff out of his window on to the grounds where no one would notice. So he slid up the sash window, lifted up the brimming chamber pot and leaned out to see where he could pour.

Unfortunately, the handle broke, and the pot fell down the side of the house, crashing through the glass conservatory roof below, smashing, and splashing its contents all over the main table where the other guests were enjoying their continental breakfast.

Without a word, the poor lad rushed into his clothes, out the front door, and hurtled along the drive in his car.

But it doesn't end there. This is the follow-up story some people tell . . .

Some time later, he concluded that his behaviour – even drunk – had been appalling, and decided to go back during the week to apologise to the lady of the house, which he did.

When he rang the sash bell, the butler came to the door, and explained that her ladyship was in a meeting at the moment, but would the young man care to wait for her in the library?

He sauntered nervously into the dull room, picked up a dusty book and sat down on the sofa. As he sat, he heard a yelp. He got up straight away and looked down to see what he'd sat on. Regrettably, it was the lady's Chihuahua, and it was now very dead.

the royal *wee*

My boss and his mate out in Windsor were keen joggers who practised regularly and always promised themselves they'd enter the London Marathon next year, but somehow their training programme never quite peaked at the right time.

One day he was tramping the woods and lanes thereabouts alone for the usual stint, a three-mile jog then a marathon ten pints. Crunching through the fallen leaves in his trainers, he felt the call of nature and knew he wouldn't make it back home to use the facilities. So he checked the coast was clear and popped behind a tree to relieve himself.

He was just shaking the drips off when he heard an irritated woman's voice behind him, saying, 'Would you mind not doing that, young man?'

And lumme if it wasn't the Queen herself, taking her corgies for their constitutional.

> She should think herself lucky he didn't turn round, standing to attention, really . . .

take *a break*

A friend of a friend, out on a shopping expedition, was in dire need of refreshment.

So, laden down with her purchases, she found a cafeteria and bought herself a refreshing cup of tea and a Kit-Kat. The place was so full the only seat she could find was opposite a scruffy punk reading the paper, but she plonked her bags down and relaxed.

Apparently, as she did so, the punk folded up his paper, reached forward for the Kit-Kat, broke off half and shoved it in his mouth.

The woman was taken aback and quite speechless, but the punk ignored her, and a minute later he picked up the rest of the bar and scoffed that as well.

By now the woman was livid. Fuming, she reached forward for the punk's cream cake, took a massive bite, then threw it back down on the table, before gathering up her bags and storming out of the cafeteria.

Still angry, she decided to catch the first bus home, felt in her pocket for her travelcard, and found her own Kit-Kat intact.

flat *season*

A friend of a friend, who is a housing officer, had to rehouse an old gypsy on the ninth floor of a block of flats.

Understandably, the old fellow wasn't too keen, but there was nowhere else for him.

After a few weeks, the housing officer started to get complaints from the old man's neighbours, not about the lift being out of action (as usual), but about a mysterious thudding and scraping occasionally coming from the new tenant's apartment. So the officer followed up the reports and went to check on the noises, but when she knocked on his door, the old bloke would only open it enough to peer out. She asked him about the noises and he explained the neighbours were always picking on him and told her to clear off – or words to that effect.

This continued for a few months. Neighbours would complain about the intolerable racket from this secretive old geezer's flat, and the housing officer would dutifully arrive on his doorstep, only to be vociferously scared away.

Apparently, the old man got so unreasonable that eventually she had to obtain a police warrant to search his flat, accompanied by officers of the law.

When he answered the door, they barged past him to the shock of their lives – neighing away in the middle of the floor surrounded by hay was the old fellow's favourite horse.

> A friend tells us that in every housing office where she's ever worked, people tell this story as having happened to a previous colleague. The only constant appears to be that it's always a gypsy. It must be the renowned love of animals that suggests the Romanies' inclusion, rather than any form of deep-seated discrimination – surely?

a friend *in need*

A friend of a friend worked in a hospice where there were two elderly bed-ridden men sharing a room.

One old chap had a bed next to a window, and would sit up and describe in loving detail to his friend the children playing in the sunshine, the dogs loping in the park and any particularly nasty street fights.

Every day there were new and amazing scenes, sketched out with such enthusiasm that although he loved the descriptions, the other old chap became sick with jealousy.

Apparently, this went on for some months, until one

night the man by the window suddenly groaned loudly and called to his friend, 'Ooh, you've got to ring for help, I don't think I'll last the night . . .'

The other fellow immediately reached for the alarm, but then thought to himself, 'If he goes, I'll get the bed by the window.'

So he lay back and, with the help of a pillow over his ears, ignored his room-mate's death-throe moaning.

In the morning, staff found the poor old bloke stiff as a board, but they reassured his companion that they'd soon have some more company for him.

'I must have the bed next to the window!' snapped the old fellow sharply. The nurses explained it would be easier if he stayed put, but he angrily insisted.

So eventually they lifted him over to the other bed. Expectantly, he levered himself up and peered out through the window – only to see a solid brick wall.

court *in the act*

A friend of a friend was a magistrate in Newcastle-upon-Tyne, and was once presiding over the case of a German sailor who was charged with being drunk and disorderly.

The unshaven tar was obviously still a little the worse for wear after his overindulgences the night before, and wasn't very coherent when it came to answering even the most basic questions. His limited grasp of English had deserted him, and none of the court officials spoke German, so he was unable to understand anything that was going on.

Recognising that this hardly constituted a fair hearing for the foreign seaman, the magistrate decided to try a different tack. So he asked if anyone in the courtroom was able to speak German.

To his relief, a thin young man in the public gallery with a rockabilly quiff raised his hand, and was ushered to the front.

The makeshift interpreter was positioned next to the defendant, and the magistrate began by asking him to find out the German's name.

Apparently, the young man turned slowly round to the defendant, his faced screwed up with severity, and screamed to the sailor at the top of his voice, 'VOT ISS YOUR NAME!!?'

> The magistrate had no choice but to charge the young man with contempt of court. Actually, that's one of those apocryphal tales that gets passed on in the family as having happened to 'Grandad' or an old uncle. Never proven, never denied, they become part of the family folklore, suitably embellished by each new generation.

a fishy *business*

A friend of a friend was throwing a swanky dinner party for her executive husband's new boss and some of the movers and shakers around town.

She had been fretting about what to serve up at such an exclusive gathering. She'd pored through all her glossiest recipe books, and woven together a tantalisingly mouth-watering menu that would have done justice to any of London's top West End restaurants.

The main course was to feature a whole poached salmon.

The king of fishes was duly purchased and the next morning the excited hostess got up especially early to lovingly prepare her *pièce de résistance*.

That evening the guests arrived fashionably late, the starter was devoured, the conversation was scintillating and the soirée was going swimmingly.

At a suitable moment, the hostess slipped away from the table to bring in the salmon from the kitchen. But she breezed through the swing doors to a horrifying sight. Her mangy cat was squatting on the work surface, tucking into the exquisitely spiced fish with great gusto.

She shooed the cat and it fled, leaving the distraught woman in a state of total panic. There was no time to prepare another dish, so she hastily disguised the damage with some judiciously placed cucumber. Then she took it through, holding it aloft to gasps of admiration.

Despite the mishap with the moggy, no one seemed to notice. The meal was acclaimed, and the hostess was complimented on her exceptional culinary skills.

But then popping back into the kitchen to set up the coffee, she noticed all was not well with the cat. In fact, the poor beast was writhing around in convulsions.

She was convinced it must be the salmon that he'd nibbled at earlier. Weighing up the pros and cons of telling the guests they'd just been poisoned, the wretched hostess finally went through and told them what had happened.

Disgusted, they all immediately rushed off to hospital and had their stomachs pumped.

The woman had only just returned home when the doorbell rang. It was the milkman. He'd tried to knock earlier, but couldn't make himself heard above the party noises.

He explained that he was just calling to see if the cat was alright.

Apparently, he'd dropped a milk crate on its head that morning.

> A version of this sick cat story was told to us by Richard Madeley, the charming presenter of ITV's justly popular *This Morning* programme, and a keen amateur urban mythologist in his own right. He claims the situation happened to his sister. After hearing that, the invitations to come and eat with Richard's family the next time we're in the area remain firmly on our mantelpieces . . .
>
> However, Richard did know an interesting variation — notably that the groggy cat is discovered after the guests have got home, so the hostess has to ring them all up and suggest the stomach pump.

the parking *incident*

The sister of a lady from down the road, beyond her salad days but still capable of freshness, had driven to the local out-of-town shopping park and was scouring the packed car park for spaces to leave her oversize, gas-guzzling metallic gold Mercedes. In one of those delicious moments, she spotted the last vacancy halfway down an aisle just before a beaten-up Beetle with two young women in it, which was rounding the corner at the far end, could stake their claim.

Swiftly establishing her precedence with a burst of speed and the wink of her indicator, the woman realised too late that her approach was all wrong. Her two young rivals in the VW hooted and waved their hands impatiently. But she was too close to the parking space in the narrow aisle and, with all the manoeuvrability of a super-tanker, had to crank the gears, blundering back and forth in order to achieve a position from where she could shoe-horn her vehicle into the space. This was too much for the fast-living youngsters. The multi-coloured Beetle revved up, streaked forward and sneaked into the parking space, missing the big Merc by millimetres and screeching to an audacious halt in the vacancy. One of the cocky young things wound down her window and sneered, 'That's what you can do when you can drive.'

The older woman showed no emotion, but slowly, deliberately, backed her car to the end of the aisle. Then she rammed her foot to the floor and, to the horror of the VW's occupants, hurtled straight down the lane, swerving at the last moment so she could slam full pelt into the Beetle, shunting it into cars in front and to the side. The two young women were speechless with shock and rage. The older woman's electric window glided slowly down.

'That's what you can do when you've got money,' she crowed, before cruising off.

> All right, all right, so you recognise that one from the film of the book *Fried Green Tomatoes at the Whistle Stop Cafe*, but several correspondents and relatives have assured us that versions of similar stories easily pre-date both book and film. This sort of literary delve into popular mythology is frequent – anyone who's seen the excellent movie *Hear My Song* will have recog-

nised the scene where the cow is almost dragged down the well by a chain attached to a heavy object as an adaptation of the classic goat story on page 21.

the dockyard *thief*

A neighbour who was a docker during the Second World War recalls the time a workmate had fallen under the suspicion of the harbour police (sometimes known as the 'river filth'). Every night at dusk, the burly fellow strolled up to the dock gate on his way home, pushing a wheelbarrow with a large grubby oil cloth draped rather dubiously over it.

This was a time of hardship and shortages, and it was feared that the bloke was half-inching some of the essential wartime supplies, which arrived daily at the port, to flog on the black market.

Every night the dock police stopped the docker at the gates and checked under the cloth for illicit goods. But the handcart was always found to be empty. Undaunted, the puzzled coppers continued with the inspection every night for weeks and weeks. But each time they lifted the cloth, the barrow was found to be bare, and the shifty docker resumed his journey home with a cheery wave.

Apparently, one enterprising young bobby, desperate to solve the case, eventually followed the docker home and watched him trundle up his back alley, open his yard gate and wheel in the barrow. When the suspect had gone indoors, the energetic PC scrambled over the backyard wall – and found 57 stolen wheelbarrows stacked up in the garden.

Another version of that criminal classic is set at a North African border checkpoint where drugs and weapons trafficking is endemic. For years a guard watches a shifty man walk through the crossing in the morning and return in the evening on a bicycle. The guard always thoroughly searches for contraband, but never finds anything. On his retirement day, the curious checkpoint charlie privately asks the part-time cyclist to let him in on his secret – what is he smuggling, and how? 'Bicycles,' is the bloke's grinning reply.

the flat*mate*

A university student was staying over with her boyfriend and stopped off at her flat *en route* to pick up some smart togs for college the next day. It was late – in fact, she checked her watch and noted it was 11.48 p.m. Then she quietly turned her key in the lock and silently switched on the lights so as not to disturb her slumbering mate. A few seconds later she was rifling through her clothes and cursing her co-habitant for the irritating habit of borrowing her best clothes without asking.

So the young woman sneaked into her friend's room and, as delicately as she could, searched through the huge pile of clothing on top of a chair. Just as she located her smart accoutrements, the poor lass accidently set off a Polaroid camera and the flash exploded in the dark. Her friend let out a groan and the woman rushed out pronto.

Later that night, there was a loud rap on the boyfriend's door. It was the police. They confirmed that the student was the woman they sought and then gently broke the news that her flatmate had been violently murdered.

Then they produced a Polaroid exposure found at the scene. The young woman took one look and blanched. It was the last snap ever taken of her friend. There stood the flatmate, trussed up, her assailant's arms clamped round her, with a hand gagging her mouth, and, nearby, a clock. It was blinking out the time: 11.59.

trunk in *charge*

Some years ago, when zoos were cruel places where animals were actually treated worse than humans (unlike today's Health Service, where humans are treated worse then animals), a family on The Great British Holiday – rain, Kiss-Me-Quick hats, chips, amusements and guaranteed 24-hour tedium – set out for a West Country zoo.

Dad pulled up in the car park, and mum and the three kids piled out of the Mini and in through the entrance.

Minutes later, the nippers were hanging off the chimps' cage, scratching their armpits and grunting (no unusual behaviour there, you might think). The parents were watching a keeper training a teenage Indian elephant to sit on a big red stool, without much success. 'He'll sit on anything red except this bloody stool,' muttered the bloke, deciding to take the errant pachyderm for a stroll instead.

After a few hours complaining about the various nose-assailing whiffs from animals and the fact that the lions, polar bears, pandas and other interesting creatures are always off apparently sleeping noisily in their dens at the other end of the compound when you want to see them, the family called it a day.

Heading wearily out of the gates, the family were struck by a commotion in the car park. The keeper they'd seen earlier was shouting to his junior jumbo to get up, but the hefty beast was refusing to do so. As they rounded a few more parked cars, the tourists were horrified to witness the scene before them: the soppy elephant had mistaken their red Mini for one of its stools, and mistakenly plonked its considerable khyber on the small car's bonnet, cruelly crushing the poor little motor.

The car was almost a write-off, but the keeper promised a quick insurance settlement – the elephant was covered, fully comprehensive.

Hobbling back to the holiday flat in the twilight, the maltreated car was rattling and scraping and soon caught the attention of the police.

When the inquisitive officers saw the damage, they enquired as to its cause. The father earnestly explained the whole sorry tale. But to no avail. The two coppers looked at one another, then one leant forward: 'D'you want to persist with this ridiculous yarn, sir, or just come clean and blow into the breathalyser?'

the maniac *on the roof*

A lass someone at college knew was travelling in her boyfriend's car late at night through the New Forest, when their car suddenly started spluttering and stalled. They'd run out of petrol in the middle of nowhere. At first she thought it might be a ruse by her bloke to get a bit of rural slap and tickle, but the concern on his face soon scotched that. It was pitch black, and the only light they could see was coming from what looked like a mansion or hospital some miles away. The boyfriend told her to lock the doors and wait while he went for help.

Hours passed, and still no sign of him. She was beginning to get very nervous. Still more time went by, when she was startled by a horrendous banging on the back, then top of the car. Before she could scream, the car was surrounded by police cars with lights flashing and sirens wailing.

A voice over a loud-hailer told her: 'Get out of the car slowly, walk steadily towards the police line, and don't, repeat don't, look around.' She did as she was told, but as she neared the police line, she couldn't stop herself looking round at the car to see what was making the awful thumping noise . . . only to see an escaped psychopath banging her boyfriend's severed head on the car roof.

the mean *machine*

Out-of-order technology

The following mechanisms have a mind of their own. It's just a shame the operators haven't. According to this workshop manual of technophobia we're prisoners of progress, and consumer goods become consumer nasties at the flick of a switch. If necessity is the mother of invention, when it comes to technology it's just the mother of all baffles.

a shocking way *to go*

Not far from Harlow there's an electrified railway and during the long summer holidays some bored kids were messing about on the line. They'd kicked their ball over the fence and gone down on to the track to retrieve it.

One kid thought it'd be funny to whip out his todger and urinate on the line to see if it made steam. His mates stood back, the kid took aim, fired, and was frazzled in a second, winkle first.

hot *hog*

A bloke my uncle knows who was mad about motorbikes recently came into some money, and decided to spend it on one of those brand new Harley Davidsons.

The bike was his pride and joy; he was always buffing it and polishing it. He even put carpet on the floor of his garage. Forever boasting about just how great his bike was, he was always on about doing a ton, MPG, cruising speed, acceleration and the like – ride to live, live to ride, etc.

One day he was having a party round his house and his friends bet him he couldn't ride his huge bike up the stairs. After a few shandies, the bloke, eager to prove them wrong, revved up his 'hog' and hurtled up the stairs. But he lost momentum halfway up and the heavy bike tumbled sideways, crushing the rider's leg. He was hauled off to hospital leaving the bike lying on its side in the kitchen.

The bloke's wife came home from the hospital and started to clear up. She mopped up the spilt petrol and, for want of somewhere better to put it, tipped the fuel down the outside lav.

A few hours later the bloke came back in the ambulance with his leg in plaster to the hip, feeling pretty dischuffed. After a cup of tea he was busting to go to the loo. But because of his leg cladding, he couldn't get up the stairs so he went outside, plonked himself down and lit a consolation fag, and the bog exploded.

over*haul*

A bloke out in the suburbs of Bristol was doing a bit of DIY, painting the outside of his house. The house was a big thirties number with a drive out the front. He had hired some ladders for the job but they were just a little too short to reach the top of the walls.

Rather than wait 'til the next weekend and hire ladders of the correct size, he racked his brain for a way to avoid spending any more money. So he threw a rope over the roof and tied it to the bumper of his car, then went around and clambered up the back of the house, tying the rope round his waist.

Unbeknown to him, his wife decided to run some errands, got into the car, revved up and dragged her hapless hubby over the house and on to the front lawn with a thump.

up *north*

An elderly London couple decided, after years of putting it off, to drive north and visit their daughter and son-in-law in Leeds.

So they got their old Ford Anglia out of the garage,

washed the accumulated dirt and cobwebs off it, and set out.

They were driving along the motorway for six hours, but still hadn't seen a signpost for Leeds. Puzzled, they resolved to ask someone in a service station.

'You're in South Mimms, mate, five miles out of London.' They'd neglected to turn off the M25.

jumbo *leak*

Some time in the seventies a Jumbo en route from Frankfurt to Rome was hijacked in mid-flight and the gun-toting terrorists demanded the plane be re-routed to Cuba. The flight crew stayed very calm, as did the passengers, even though the hijackers were screaming at them and waving their pistols around.

After a little while, when it was clear the flight crew were going to bluff them out, the terrorists – or freedom fighters, depending on your views – became very agitated. One of them started an altercation with a passenger, who bravely shouted back at him and squared up to him, fists raised. But the hijacker went spare and, in a moment of madness, fired his gun at the passenger, a huge German who obviously enjoyed his sausages and beer.

The bullet missed and shot through the plane's fuselage, causing a large hole and immediate decompression. The trigger-happy terrorist was sucked through the hole like a piece of spaghetti, and all the other passengers were ripped out of their seat by the force, as the plane spiralled out of control.

But the second person to be dragged towards the hole was the portly German. Luckily, he arrived at the gaping chasm bottom first — a part of his body amply equipped to stop him slipping any further — and completely plugged the gap. Normal oxygen supply was resumed, the plane came out of its spin and was able to land normally, and the remaining hijacker was arrested at the airport.

As for the hero, he was given a reward but treated for severe frostbite of the buttocks.

cashpoint *Charlie*

A jack-the-lad was out on the ale in London's Piccadilly area. When the pubs had closed, he strolled down to Charing Cross to catch his train home, but was gripped by the pressing need for sustenance. Checking his pocket, he found he had just about £1.80. It was a stark choice: home to Morden or a quarterpounder with all the trimmings. Then he remembered his flexible friend, his credit card!

So he swiftly nipped into a Burger Bar and had already started scoffing his flame-grilled patties when he reached the cashpoint. He put in his card, set his snack down next to the keypad, punched in his P.I.N. and waited for the cash to come rolling out. But the screen flashed up: 'SORRY, YOU HAVE USED THE WRONG PERSONAL NUMBER. DO YOU WISH TO TRY AGAIN?'

A bit flustered, he keyed in another number. Same message. Not a little fazed, he took stock and settled himself to try again. Convinced the first number was right and that he'd just keyed it in wrong, he carefully pressed the number again.

But when he finished, the screen flashed that his card had been retained, and the glass shield came grinding down, sadly locking away his delicious burger.

a low *note*

One of our old dinner ladies from school was chattering on the corner of a heavily parked-up busy road when she saw a flaky driver, veering from side to side, prang a stationary motor.

Expecting the driver to carry on regardless, as so many people seem to do in this day and age, she and others in the street were pleasantly surprised to see the considerate driver stop, earnestly examine the damage and take a pen and paper from his car and write down the details. He then placed the note under the damaged car's windscreen wiper before driving on.

A minute later, the owner of the damaged car appeared. He was distressed to see his dented wing but pleased to see the note, which he read carefully.

Then he exploded. The passer-by said she'd witnessed the accident and asked what the matter was: didn't he have the other driver's details on the note?

'See for yourself,' muttered the angry owner, showing her the paper, which read:

'I've just crunched your car, and because there are loads of nosy people watching me, I'm pretending to write down my name, registration number and insurance details.'

the surprise *package*

A woman in her mid-thirties had suffered from a rare bowel complaint and had to undergo pioneering surgery for the implanting of a mechanical sphincter.

The device allowed the bowels to be opened and closed by the passing of a magnet over a sensor placed in her chest, and although odd proved to be very effective. Until, that is, one day the unfortunate woman was jetting off for a fortnight in the sun, and happened to pass through the airport security scan.

It wasn't until she sat down in her window seat that she realised that the airport scanners obviously use magnetism as well . . .

> Apparently shop security devices have been known to have a similar effect, usually on people leaving without paying 'by accident'.

wrong *ring*

A friend of a former colleague told me about an incident that recently befell his boss on a train. He was feeling chuffed at claiming a four-seat table for himself and settled down to a nice quiet journey reading his book. The whistle blew and as the train lurched away, a loud, acne-ed yuppie trousered his way into the carriage, threw his bags down on the table, collapsed into the seat opposite, and immediately brandished his portable phone and began a loud, oafish conversation – 'buy . . . sell . . . take a rain-check . . . hyper!' . . . – that sort of thing.

The quieter man couldn't believe his misfortune and tried to ignore the boorish city type, but he was so noisy, ringing people up and rustling papers and shouting 'Yah . . . yah . . . yah . . .' into the phone all the time, that the bloke couldn't take any more and set off with his stuff for another part of the train.

He'd just sat down when an old man opposite him went pale and groaned. He was having a heart attack and collapsed on the floor. The guard arrived as passengers tried to come to the old gent's aid, and he explained that they'd have to wait 'til the next station before they could phone as the train's communication lines were down.

'I know someone with a phone!' said the bloke happily. 'We can ring ahead and have an ambulance waiting for him at the station.'

So the guard, the bloke and some other concerned passengers marched triumphantly back down the carriage. The yuppie was still in mid-conversation when the guard cut in to explain the situation and ask him, as it was an emergency, if they might have the use of his portable phone.

At first the yuppie waved them away as if he was busy, still talking down the line. But when they persisted and got increasingly agitated, he threw the phone down, went the colour of beetroot and looking down mumbled, 'You can't. It's only a fake phone.'

charge of *the light brigade*

My old geography teacher told me about some friends of his who decided to get out of the rat race and moved to the Cornish coast. They bought a lovely ivy-covered cottage right out on a peninsular miles from any town. The only building nearby was the local lighthouse.

They had a fabulous time away from it all, without a care in the world. Until their electricity bill landed with a thud on the mat. The amount they owed was astronomical for such a tiny cottage. In fact, it ran into thousands of pounds.

Horrified, the couple rang the Electricity Board, who came to investigate, and discovered that the light in the lighthouse was actually running off their domestic supply.

mexican *waves*

A Mexican cook who'd been working in a run-down service station on the M4 for four months was taken ill one morning just as he was starting his shift.

He wasn't very reliable anyway, and when he complained of burning stomach pains, the supervisor only reluctantly agreed to let him drive to the nearest hospital some miles away, and warned him to be back soon, or he'd be given the big heave-ho.

After four hours, the cook still hadn't returned, so the maddened supervisor rang up the hospital where the Mexican had said he'd go, to see if he'd turned up there.

To his surprise, after a brief conversation with the casualty department, a specialist came on the phone and asked if the cook ever had to use a microwave.

'Yes, he does,' said the supervisor.

'And is it an old one?'

'Well, yes, one of the earlier models, why?'

'Stop using it immediately!' urged the consultant. 'The rays have been escaping, and your chef's kidneys have been cooked through.'

cow *down below!*

A fax salesman who's forever pestering us on the phone was tooling up the A1 one gorgeous sunny day in his ace new cerise Mazda convertible.

He was having a magic time: shades on, Springsteen blasting out, rag-top down, catching some rays.

Then out of the blue a huge black and white Friesian cow landed in the back seat with a bone-crunching thud.

47

He careered over to the hard shoulder and tried to remove the poor dead beast, but it was unbelievably heavy and stuck fast. So he drove off the main road to the nearest village and found the local garage.

Once they'd stopped laughing, the grease monkeys managed to lift the cow out with an engine hoist, but the car was covered in unspeakable muck.

Before he could face the rest of the journey, the driver nipped into the local pub for a stiffener.

Inside, he got talking to the publican and related his story.

As he did, another drinker piped up. 'You must have been below me,' he laughed. 'I just ploughed my lorry into a herd of cows on the bridge over the A1.'

state *of shock*

It was rush hour in the City and all the London tubes were jammed solid. A middle-aged rum-pot who'd enjoyed an extended publisher's lunch bustled his way to the front of the platform. Luckily there was no train approaching, because the fogey jostled just a little too much. He missed his footing and tumbled on to the electrified track, receiving a dreadful shock that sounded like a thunder clap.

The megavolt charge knocked him unconscious, and rush-hour people were screaming and fainting at the horror of it all. The marvellous emergency services arrived swiftly and in no time the bloke was back on his feet, apparently none the worse for wear. Until, that is, a smiling tube worker gave the unfortunate fellow a friendly pat on the back – and both his arms, amputated and cauterised by the shock, fell on to the platform.

caught *in the headlights*

A friend of my uncle is a retired carpenter who lives up on the edge of the Pennines.

He drove a lovely old polished Rover of an evening and regularly toured up to his local in the hills where they don't know the meaning of closing time. The bloke didn't overindulge, and usually left just before eleven.

But practically every night as he drove back along an unlit and particularly winding stretch of road, two grebos on monster bikes spitting horsepower would really put the willies up him.

The huge greasers, headlights blazing, would take up the whole road, coming the opposite way. They blazed towards him with no thought for road safety, playing chicken and forcing him to swerve off the road into hedges to avoid crashing.

This situation went on for some time. Then one night, the bloke was driving back with a little more Dutch courage than usual coursing through his veins.

He spotted the bikers a few bends ahead.

Slamming his foot down, he hammered along the switchback road thinking this time he'd show them who's boss.

He rounded the last corner into the glare of the bikers' two headlights and thundered for the gap between them – too late realising the headlights actually belonged to an articulated lorry.

> There's a distinct similarity there to another 'worm turning' bikers story, in which a driver in a motorway cafe is harassed by a chapter of Hell's Angels while eating his dinner. They stub their fags out in his fried egg and generally humiliate him, but he doesn't retaliate, just walks slowly out. 'Not much of a man, was he?' sneers one of the bikers. 'Not much of a driver, either,' observes the waitress. 'He's just driven his truck over a row of motorbikes.'

hidden *extras*

A friend of a friend's hubby knew a bargain when he saw one, and he was looking at one right now. He had been scouring the papers for a runaround for his little woman but to date anything decent had cost more than he could afford. But, as he'd always reckoned, the car auctions had come up trumps. There it was, a nifty little hatchback, with not too many miles on the clock, full MOT and a car alarm sticker to boot. It had even taken a magnet on every part of the bodywork except the windows.

Only one dodgy point: apparently it had been in a nasty smash. But you'd never know that to look at it. Couldn't get better value for love nor money and he'd tried both on more than one occasion.

A scratch of the nose, a tug of the ear and it was his. Cash on the nail and home to the missus. His wife was chuffed to pieces with her present and strapped hubby in for a spin out to the nearby countryside, stopping on the way at one of humanity's new cathedrals – an out-of-town shopping centre.

They were just nearing the top of one of those tummy-churning hills when the wife was dazzled by the warm glow of the golden evening sun. She pulled down the sun visor on her side, and an eyeball and a severed finger dropped out into her lap.

motorway *deliverance*

A middle-aged man from Kidderminster couldn't believe his luck when he was driving past Birmingham on the M5 and there was virtually no other traffic on the road – and no rozzers either. Not one to miss exploiting any opportunity in his company car, the bloke was toeing it through the tarmac bedlam that is the area's road system.

But as he was storming round the bend of a flyover, he lost control of his Sierra, which hit the wall, flipped over and came to rest in a horrifying smash on the hard shoulder. The car was clearly a write-off, but miraculously the driver emerged virtually unscathed and absolutely elated at his good fortune.

Just to be on the safe side he quickly hopped over the barrier to avoid any more danger. Unfortunately, on the other side of the barrier was a 30 foot drop to another dual carriageway below. The poor bloke plummeted down and landed in the fast lane, where sadly he was run over by a Post Office van.

pull the *other one*

Some years back, a widowed friend of my mum from the local historical society in Ramsbottom decided to fritter away some of her deceased husband's hard-earned cash and splash out on a lovely pale green Morris Minor to visit the grandchildren. There was only one problem: she couldn't drive. So she duly invested a little more of her lump sum in some lessons and passed with flying colours at the fifth time of asking.

Normally Morris Minors are the most reliable cars on the road, but she reckoned hers must have been a real Friday car. Not only was it impossible to start in summer, but the car drank petrol like there was no tomorrow and kangarooed everywhere, leaving acrid clouds of thick white smoke in its wake.

What with the fuel bills and taking it to the garage the whole time, it really seemed like her runaround was giving her the runaround. The oddest thing of all was that the garage could never find anything wrong with the vehicle.

One day, when the car had been in for the umpteenth time that month, a wily mechanic who was determined to find her driving at fault, asked the old lady to take him for a spin round the houses to see if he could spot anything unusual. Happy to oblige, the sprightly old blue rinse hopped into the driver's seat, carefully put on her safety belt, then pulled out the choke knob as far as it would go and hung her handbag on it . . . solving the mystery once and for all.

Another favourite mechanic's yarn concerns a woman who keeps complaining of an infuriating rattle in her motor. But, as usual, all garage tests prove fruitless. Eventually, one of the mechanics visits her unawares at home and discovers that she had been keeping loose change in her glove compartment, but removing the money before letting the grease monkeys loose on her car because she doesn't trust them.

quite *a climax*

A health and safety consultant heard about a firm in the same line of business who were commissioned to make a video pinpointing the dos and don'ts of modern forklift truck driving.

After some initial research they elected to shoot the film in a busy factory that had a large loading area beetling with forklifts, right next to the canal. When approached the firm were only too willing to cooperate. They were proud of their safety record and made only one condition, insisting that the film would stress in no uncertain terms that none of their employees had ever been involved in any forklift accident of any kind.

The script was written and passed by the management.

They were particularly impressed at the climactic catastrophe, featuring a loopy forklift driver and a fateful brush with the canal. The scene featured a stunt driver careering around the compound with a full pallet, then leaping from the machine just before it tumbled into the murky depths of the polluted water.

The day of filming dawned and the first few takes went swimmingly. With the bulk of the drama in the can, the excited crew set up for the climax. They checked again that every precaution had been taken. A crane and professional diver were on stand-by to retrieve the unlucky forklift. Just a few final tweaks and the stuntman climbed into the hot seat.

The cameras rolled and to everyone's delight the scene went like a dream: the forklift driver from hell hurtled around the yard breaking every rule in the book, skidded towards the canal and only just escaped by the skin of his teeth, the stand-in driver leaping free as the plummeting vehicle plunged over the quayside.

Swiftly dispatched with a crane hook to hoist the forklift back on to dry land, the diver disappeared from sight. The crew were still slapping the stuntman on the back and praising his screencraft when the frogman's head popped out of the waterway.

'Which one do you want?' he spluttered. 'There's three down here already.'

Forklift trucks are notoriously tricky to handle. One of the authors once personally demolished one of those retail skyscrapers made of cola cans while attempting a complicated reverse triple salko manoeuvre – not entirely on purpose, it must be said – and spent the rest of the day restacking the fizzing time-bombs in shame.

wash *day blues*

A sobbing man phoned the complaints department of a large store to protest that his brand-new washing machine had gone berserk and wrecked his kitchen. His was a sorry tale spluttered out between sobs.

It seemed that the very first time he loaded the washer with laundry, it had gone into a violent mechanical frenzy, smashing his worktop in two as it cannoned up and down, before hammering across the tiles to demolish a run of cupboards. Then the motorised monster savaged the fridge so badly that the door ended up permanently jammed shut.

The astonished customer relations manager could hardly believe his ears. The type of washing machine in question was one of the most popular and reliable brands. How could such a thing have happened? Astronomical compensation figures swirled before his eyes as he breathlessly implored the customer to explain exactly how this bizarre and disturbing incident came about.

The fastidious customer had carefully followed the installation instructions. He naturally started at number one which read 'Remove all packaging'. This, he confessed, had been quite a struggle. The first bit had seemed simple enough: two layers of cardboard, then bubble wrap, followed by tape, plastic wedges and a few metal plates.

'But then came the tricky part,' said the householder indignantly. 'I had to resort to a hammer and chisel to remove that huge lump of concrete underneath.'

the appliance *of science*

The consumer complaints department of a notable electrical retail store received an irate call from a distraught woman claiming that her recently purchased vacuum cleaner had exploded and demolished her kitchen.

The customer services manager tried her best to placate the tearful caller, explaining that she'd never before heard of such an occurrence. Personally, she found it difficult to believe such an incident was possible. She had been in the electrical business long enough to know that most nasty accidents with household appliances (especially vacuum cleaners) involved single men or Tory MPs. The caller reasserted the validity of her claim and explained the chain of events leading to the catastrophe.

She'd been cleaning the kitchen when a mouse shot out from under the skirting boards. Quick as a flash the woman aimed her nozzle and sucked the poor creature thudding into the dust bag. That was that, or so she thought, until she switched off the appliance, when she heard the ensnared rodent scrabbling about in a desperate bid for freedom.

The woman was mortified but again inspiration came in a flash. She turned on a gas ring, positioned the vacuum hose over the source and subjected the household pest to a severe gassing.

But when she switched off the vacuum cleaner the mouse was still defying her, scratching feebly. It obviously needed more gas. So she flicked the switch again. It must have caused a tiny spark and . . .

the driving *dog*

A fella I worked with reckons his American uncle was banned from driving for being over the limit, but was mad on cars and liked his drink. So he bought an automatic and taught his St Bernard dog to drive. The dog would steer, and he would manipulate the other controls using a driving school dual-control facility. He even applied for a provisional driver's licence for the dog under the name Henry St Bernard as a joke. But it paid off, and the dog became something of a familiar and popular figure in the small town, driving his master to the shops or a bar. After a little while, though, the highway police stopped and arrested them. But there was such a public outcry that the charges were dropped and the man got off with a simple warning. Henry the dog didn't get off so lightly: he was fined $50 for driving after dark on a provisional licence . . .

hitched *up*

Two New Age travellers went to Bristol to look at an old ambulance advertised in the paper. It was no good, and they decided to hitch back to the south Devon moor where they lived.

They were so rank looking that they were standing on the bend of the road for hours without any driver so much as looking at them.

Then a late model hatchback slowed down in front of them, and they swiftly took up the offer, jumping in – one in the back next to a pile of Sainsbury's bags, the other in the front passenger seat. The woman driver stiffly asked them where they wanted to go. They explained where they lived, but said they'd settle for halfway as it was such a long distance.

As it was, the driver seemed eager to please them and drove them all the way to Haldon Moor, but without saying a word – they assumed she'd just passed her test and didn't want any distractions, so they just gave her appropriate directions.

An hour later, they arrived at the travellers' destination. The woman looked visibly relieved when they got out and thanked them for 'not attacking her'. The two lads looked puzzled, and thanked her profusely for the lift. 'Lift?' said the woman. 'But I thought you were hijacking me!'

a nasty *set-to*

When my uncle left the Paras, one of his mates got a job for a building company driving a huge cement mixer truck.

Driving the diesel-guzzling concrete monster thrilled

him to bits, but working on big ready-mix jobs often kept him away from home for days at a time. And although he loved his young wife dearly, he became convinced she was having an affair. It was the little things: she'd started wearing skimpy tops and too much perfume.

Apparently, in an effort to catch her out, he drove home early one day. Sure enough, there was a flash red soft-top sports car parked outside the house, and the upstairs curtains were closed.

Wiping a tear from his eye with his fist, he backed up his truck, and filled the convertible to the brim with quick setting cement.

Job done, he trundled round the corner to see what would happen. He'd just hauled on the handbrake when a skinny bloke nipped out of the house, hopped on his hidden bike and wobbled off down the road.

An alternative, slightly less misogynist ending to the above yarn has the wife in tears because the hubby's mistaken jealousy has ruined the brand-new car she'd bought him as a surprise present. Apparently she had been secretly working as a barmaid in the evenings to afford the treat and bought the car from her earnings. The man she is in the house with turns out to be the salesman who has just delivered the motor.

mythellaneous

Scientific

* Colouring the rim of a compact disc, or freezing it, improves the sound quality (except those by Phil Collins)

* Record shops play everything faster to make it sound more exciting

* Arsenal's games at Highbury are so incredibly tedious that at one stage during a particularly bad match, the big screen began showing a film. (On another occasion, it screened Open University programmes)

* New shopping malls puff different smells through their air conditioning to make you feel good and spend more money

* Radar sterilises sailors

* Bored air traffic controllers see how close they can make planes fly without causing a crash

* A US university once lost lucrative research work for a huge agribusiness multi-national by wiping a file on its mainframe the professors thought was a student joke – it was called 'rat-penis-data'

* 40 per cent of automobile accidents occur in car parks

* New programmes in all software packages make a note of consumer habits of users and send them back to manufacturers

* Wrap your phone cards in cling film to recharge them

the long *arm of the law*

―――

Scams and scamsters

Crime doesn't pay ... enough. Judge for yourself. This roll call of scams and scamsters points the finger at those who have a stab at the things we'd all secretly love to get away with. But if you're dumb enough to try some of the ill-conceived schemes here, remember: ignorance really is no defence.

fat filly foils *felony*

I've never found out exactly who this happened to, but I have my suspicions that it was a teacher friend of the woman that told me.

Anyway, the woman involved in the story was extremely large, stout, portly, big-boned, call it what you will. One day she popped down to her building society in Exeter and was just squeezing through the revolving doors when she noticed there was a hold-up in progress.

The two inexperienced bandits threw everyone into a blind panic by waving shotguns around and screaming at the customers to get out, including the large lady. They proceeded to force the staff to hand over all the cash, then told them to get down and stay down on the floor 'til they were well away.

But when they turned to make their getaway they found the big lass sweating and in a right fluster, stuck fast in the revolving doors. The villains grabbed her and tried to force her through, then pull her out, but she was jammed and so were the doors. Shooting her wouldn't have done much good, and there was no other way out. They were trapped, like trapped rats in a rat trap for rats.

A few minutes later the police arrived – complete with a man carrying a blow-torch to free the humiliated lady – and arrested the crooks.

Ironically, although the lady was in all the papers and offered a large reward by the building society, she was too embarrassed to attend the presentation ceremony.

backwards in the *fast lane*

The boss of a friend had been out in town one night living it up in a champagne bar. He stumbled out into his Porsche in the wee small hours and set off home via the M25. There were no other cars about and the fat cat put his foot to the floor, soon reaching a ton.

He was enjoying himself so much that he missed his turning, and, this being a motorway, the next junction was miles away. Screeching to a halt, and checking to see if anything was behind in the dark, he decided to risk backing up to his turning in the outside lane.

He slammed the car into reverse, stamped down hard on the accelerator and careered backwards. Then SMASH! An Escort XR3i had ploughed straight into him. The police arrived immediately and rushed up to the other driver.

The Porsche driver was fretting, thinking he'd be breath-alysed and get a life ban or something. After a short time one of the officers walked towards him. He felt his heart flutter.

'Scuse me, sir, but have you had a few jars tonight at all?' asked the officer.

'Yes, I have to admit I have had a little to drink,' confessed the driver, expecting the worst.

Then the officer leaned forward conspiratorially and said, 'I shouldn't worry about it mate, the other driver's so ratted he thinks you were reversing in the fast lane.'

blue light *spells danger*

A workmate's uncle was driving home one evening along a busy urban ring road. The thing is, he was so drunk he could hardly stand, and he shouldn't have been sitting in a car, let alone driving one. He was crawling along the inside lane of the dual carriageway trying not to draw attention to himself. But he was going so slowly (with the occasional sidelong weave) that his driving had the opposite effect, and he was soon pulled over by the law.

They took one look at his rolling oyster eyes and caught one whiff of his breath, and 'suggested' he abandon his car and accompany them to the station. They were just about to take him away when two cars had a smash on the other side of the central reservation. The coppers warned the inebriated uncle to stay put and dashed over.

But spotting his chance to make his escape during the commotion, he jumped into action. Making sure the coppers didn't see him, he sped home as fast as he could. He drove straight into the garage and ran inside, telling his startled wife: 'If the police come round, I've been ill all day with a cold, haven't been out, haven't used the car and I'm asleep in bed, OK?' Then he picked up a bottle of whisky and wobbled off to bed.

Half an hour later the police turned up. The wife answered the door, and blurted out, 'He's been ill all day, hasn't used the car, and is asleep now,' before they'd even asked anything. 'In that case you won't mind if we take a look in your garage, madam,' said one officer, and she sheepishly handed over the keys.

As they opened the door, the wife gasped. There, to the officers' obvious satisfaction, was a police car, with the radio blaring out and the blue light still flashing away.

'this is a *pick-up!*'

A workmate's son is a motorcycle courier. One day he received a call for a wait-and-return job to go from an address in King's Cross to a large bank in the middle of London, and back to King's Cross again. The biker nipped through the heavy traffic to the pick-up place and collected a small brown envelope and a holdall, which he put in his pannier, and headed off for the bank.

He arrived at the bank, propped up his bike and went inside, handing over the envelope to a cashier as directed. Within seconds of the woman reading the note, alarms went off all over the joint, and the place was crawling with gun-toting security guards.

The courier, standing in his full garb – leathers, skid lid and radio stuttering away – was so stunned he couldn't speak. Later, in the police station, they showed him the note that had been in the envelope.

It read: 'Fill the bag with money. I've got a gun, and I'm not afraid to use it.'

signed, *sealed and delivered*

The father of a bloke I went to school with was a sergeant in the Sweeney – or so he said – and was once called out to the scene of an armed robbery, a high street bank.

The teller explained a shifty-looking bloke in a trench-coat had entered the bank, come over to his window and shoved a dog-eared envelope under the glass.

The bank clerk squinted at the childish scrawl on the back of the envelope. The note read, 'GIV US ALL THE MUNNY, IVE GOT A GUN.'

He looked up to find himself staring point-blank down the barrel of a shaking pistol. Normally a stickler for company guidelines, the teller complied immediately, thrusting wads of tenners over the counter, which the robber thrust into his greedy holdall.

Meanwhile, the thief himself had just arrived home and started excitedly to count his booty, when the police burst through the door bristling with automatic weapons.

The robber threw his arms in the air immediately, but was baffled by the efficiency of the police on the case. 'How did you track me down so fast?' he wailed.

'Quite simple, Mastermind,' the sergeant sneered, snapping on the bracelets. 'Your name and address were on the other side of the envelope.'

crisp *business*

A small crisp factory in the Midlands was suffering from such a cashflow crisis that they could barely even afford to buy the spuds that were their lifeblood.

Then in a flash of brilliance one young shopfloor scamster hit upon a wizard scheme to save the day. Without wasting any time, the company acted on his initiative and launched a high-profile nationwide 'Interesting Potato' competition, asking entrants to send them as many funny-shaped, comical, odd or lewdly-knobbled spuds as they could.

Strangely, there was no prize given out. But all the entries were turned into crisps and the factory made a small fortune.

foul *play*

A mate who began work in Docklands during the construction explosion of the eighties was regaled with the story of one of his predecessors who laboured in the area when it was still used to offload goods from the world's ships, and not to load the wallets of the world's shits.

Apparently, this young apprentice also played for the works football team, and one Saturday, in a particularly rough match with another dockers' team, he was clobbered with a studs-up tackle by the opposition's hatchet man for being flash.

Writhing in agony, the players soon realised that the lad's shin was badly broken. One docker immediately began to run for an ambulance, but some of the older, wiser lags had a better idea and called him back.

They got the wounded boy standing again, helped him home, and told him to hold his leg until Monday, which he did. When Monday arrived, they carried him painfully into work, placed him at the bottom of a big grain silo, and ran for the foreman, claiming the lad was the victim of an industrial accident.

It worked – and the young man received £10,000 in compensation.

take *the tube*

An old friend now living in London used to run a pub in Dublin. It was a typically lively, bustling bar where the crack was always good and the Guinness flowed like – well, like Guinness in a Dublin bar really.

Anyhow, one day, after a particularly heavy lunchtime

session, the landlord went to switch on the racing and noticed to his dismay that the TV had been stolen from its shelf up on the wall. Straight away he got on the blower to the 'Gards' and within a few minutes two officers arrived.

Officiously noting down various interior details, the sergeant finally approached the landlord and asked where the goggle box was when it was stolen.

The landlord pointed to the empty shelf high up on the wall.

'Well, it's people like you who make our job impossible,' groaned the sergeant. 'Fancy leaving an expensive article like that out where everyone can see it.'

an unfair *cop*

A friend's dad is a desk sergeant in the West Midlands Constabulary. Although his job these days is a long way from the frontline in the fight against crime, in his younger days he pounded the beat around Handsworth.

This was well before the days of joyriders, ramraiders and serial killers: criminals in those days were an altogether nicer breed. At the time one of his colleagues had an interesting experience. The copper was patrolling a particularly ill-lit street. With his torch blazing, he flashed into each doorway and ginnel, weeding out the homeless and stopping every black BMW he saw, and generally keeping 'em peeled.

It was just as well, because his vigilance soon paid off. The flashlight illuminated the front of a cosy old tobacconist's with the door slightly ajar.

Steeling himself for possible violent confrontation, he slowly pushed open the door. Nothing appeared to be

amiss, so radioing the station the flatfoot poked around the shop. Then he checked no one was looking and helped himself to 200 cigarettes, which he hid under his helmet.

The flustered shopowner arrived shortly, bursting with gratitude, and after checking his goods he praised the policeman's diligence and dedication to the job. Then he insisted on giving the officer a little 'thank you' for his trouble. 'Here, take these two hundred ciggies,' he offered.

'No, no, sir, that really won't be necessary, I'm only doing my job,' the bobby protested uncomfortably. 'Anyway, I don't have anywhere to put them.'

'Nonsense,' replied the shopkeeper, reaching up. 'You can hide them under your helmet.'

blue *murder*

A small-time Cardiff TV company a friend used to work for was very excited one day when they landed something of a scoop. There had been a grisly death of a woman in the locality and the chief of police in Wales had agreed to be interviewed for HTV – a very rare occurrence, and one which showed how seriously the law was taking the crime.

The hand-picked outside broadcast crew arrived on location, set up, and respectfully greeted the stuffy big-wig, who was clearly deeply affected by what he'd witnessed in the house.

The interview was understandably solemn as the police chief relayed the details of the horrible death in a dignified monotone:

'Several parts of the woman's body, including the head, were found by officers in the fridge; both legs and one arm were discovered in the potting shed, and the bulk of the torso was uncovered by police digging in the flower beds,' explained the pallid chief.

At the end of the interview, the producer thanked him in hushed tones, and the crew stood in respectful silence.

All except the sound engineer, that is, who immediately chirruped: 'So you've ruled out suicide then?'

radio *daze*

New York is the citiest of cities and you either love it or loathe it; either way, you have to respect the resourcefulness and spunk of its inhabitants. Take the case of a friend from Scunthorpe who moved out to Manhattan to work as a social worker. His job took him to some of the roughest parts of town – Hell's Kitchen, the Bronx, the Stretford End – and he would invariably take his car, a little Honda, with him. And every so often, the dinky motor would be broken into, side window smashed, car stereo half-inched, and speakers wrenched from the doors.

Having lost three sound systems in this way, the honest bloke decided not to bother with the in-car vibes anymore. But mindful of the inquisitiveness of the local youth, he fashioned a sign reading, in vivid red, 'NO CAR STEREO', and stuck it on the inside of the passenger window.

Thus fortified, he set off on a visit as usual, parking in the housing precinct of one of his clients. An hour later, he emerged from the apartment and strolled over to his wheels, but was dismayed to see that, despite the sign, someone had still smashed in the windows.

The sign was still there, though, lying on the passenger seat. Picking it up, even the disgruntled bloke had to laugh when he saw it: next to 'NO CAR STEREO', the cheeky intruder had scrawled 'JUST CHECKING'.

court *out*

A barrister representing the husband in a divorce settlement had been brought in at the last minute and wasn't too *au fait* with the case, so as soon as he arrived in court he asked the defendant to fill in his financial details on a sheet of paper so he could show them to the district judge.

This was swiftly done and returned just as they entered the chamber. The barrister quickly read the completed form with a little dismay. On the 'income' column, the bloke had filled in what he earned from his part-time work, added income support and tallied it at the bottom – it really was a pittance. Perhaps understandably, he had scribbled next to the column 'F. ALL'.

Proceedings began and, as expected, the stuffy judge suggested that to save time they could skip the cross-examination and complete the formalities on paper. The barrister, recognising that the use of the vernacular might scupper his chances, demurred, saying it would be just as quick to take oral evidence.

The judge didn't want to hear that, and requested that he be able to see the means statement of the husband.

The barrister stalled. 'Well, er . . .'

'You do have the completed statement, do you not?'

'Yes.'

'Well, then, I should like you to present it to the court.'

'We would rather not,' continued the defence brief, 'as it includes a colloquialism that may prejudice my client's case.'

'What sort of colloquialism?' queried the judge.

'I'd really rather not say.'

'Come come,' said the judge. 'We're all broad-minded people. Pipe up! What does it say?'

'Er, well . . . it says "F. ALL", sir.'

' "F. ALL"?'

'It's an expletive, m'lud.'

'Yes, yes, but what does it mean?'

The barrister hesitated a moment, before gathering himself and thundering, 'It means "fuck all", your honour.'

At which point the wife's solicitor leaned forward and, in a stage whisper, declared, ' "Family Allowance", you idiot.'

motorway *madness*

The M57 traffic police received a number of calls from extremely distressed motorists and set out to apprehend a maniac driver who had being putting the willies up his fellow motorway users. After a long chase they pulled a bloke over who'd been hammering down the outside lane at 100 m.p.h., ignoring the traffic, looking backwards out of his side window with a hideous grimace on his face and terrifying other motorists.

It turned out that the fiend was actually keeping his eyes dutifully on the road, and had a mask with 'the face of the living idiot' strapped to the back of his head to scare the pants off other road users. Regrettably this particular form of errant behaviour is not against the law and the police were forced to let the crackpot driver off, scot free (except for a speeding ticket).

a dead *halt*

An acquaintance of a country doctor from East Sussex had a crony with a very peculiar monicker, to wit Dr Ezekiel De'Ath, and was being driven home by this gentleman on one dark rainy winter's night. Suddenly a bobby on the beat stepped out into the beam of the headlights, arm raised in the routine fashion.

'Excuse me, sir,' intoned the constable, 'could I see your licence?'

'Certainly, officer,' replied the driver.

'Ah,' said the copper, clocking the name, Dr De'Ath. 'I'm so glad I stopped you, sir. We've been trying to keep you off the road for years.'

crimebotch *UK*

The owner of a sub-post office in Surrey was approached one day by researchers from the BBC's *Crimewatch UK* advising him that they would shortly be filming some dramatic robbery reconstruction scenes at a bank up the road in his small town, and that he shouldn't be unduly worried about what he saw.

On the allotted day, the film crew arrived and set everything up, and the jobbing actors were trying their hardest to sound tough as old boots – none too convincingly, it must be said – as they put their make-up on.

Filming began and crowds gathered to watch the spectacle – nothing had ever happened like this in the town before – and the town square looked like a Chinese fire drill. The preliminary scenes in the can, the crew took a lunchtime break and all trotted off to the pub for some liquid nosebag.

During this period, the postmaster, who'd been kept informed of the television crew's progress by customers, was approached by another BBC researcher. The shell-suited young man explained that the bank involved in the original raid wouldn't look good enough on the telly, so he wondered if the postmaster would mind if they filmed a few short scenes inside his shop. The owner readily agreed.

A few minutes later two actors, balaclava-ed and tooled up to look like gunmen, burst through the door, pointed their Uzis at the postmaster, threatened him and demanded he hand over all the cash. Grinning and commenting that they'd arrived a little hastier than he'd expected – he regretted he hadn't had time to tidy up – the postmaster continued to make small talk as he gathered and bagged up the morning's takings, and handed the loot over to the thespian felons. The rogue pair turned on their heels and fled as quickly as they'd arrived, not even leaving the receipt he'd asked for.

Ten minutes later, the three men with cameras, leads and microphones came into the post office and asked where the power points were, followed by the director. The postmaster asked him why they needed power now – surely they'd acted out the scene just now?

The crew looked sheepish, and the director went pale.

'Not again,' he moaned. 'All our actors are still boozing it up at the bar. I'm sorry to tell you those were genuine robbers. And this is the second time in this series that someone's done that to us.'

Don't have nightmares, will you, Mr Ross.

myth_ellaneous_

Legal

* Manufacturers could make cars that were impossible to break into and steal, but they won't do it because write-offs help sales

* With a telephone card and a teaspoon, a talented thief can infiltrate any establishment in the country

* There's a code you can punch in on your telephone that will make all your calls free from then on. When people are caught doing it, they're charged with another crime and it's all hushed up

* Buy stamps with '1st Class' on them now and because of inflation they'll be worth millions in years to come

* Music-loving Colombians are furious at a drug smuggler who pressed cocaine into a record and got caught by customs at Heathrow – every record coming in from the country is now split open

* Before the Prime Minister visited a national newspaper recently, police sniffer dogs found no guns or explosives – but a huge stash of marijuana in the toilets

* If you want to hide the corpse after a murder, give it to a pig. They eat the lot – even the toenails

food *and drink*

Half-baked hiccups

Eat, drink and be wary. The daily bread's mouldy, the milk
of human kindness is curdled, and even the pint that thinks
it's a quart isn't quite so sure any more. A gut-rotting
helping of scare-stories and indigestible suggestions, spiced
up with lashings of sauce . . .

the office party *and Mr Byrite*

A straight-laced, hen-pecked office worker in London's West End attended his Xmas office party in the afternoon, but rather overdid it with the drinks, made a complete nonce of himself and ended up being violently sick all over his clothes.

Realising that his garb was ruined, but not wanting to miss his train to Brighton, he nipped down to Mr Byrite on Oxford Street for some new clobber.

In the shop, he spent about two minutes choosing the stuff, throwing it in a pile on the till as he went, and then hurriedly paid for it.

He just about caught his train, and rushed straight for the toilet, tearing off his stinking damp trousers, shirt and jacket and recklessly throwing them out of the train window.

Then he opened the bag to put on his new clothes, and discovered to his dismay, that all he had in there was some socks, a T-shirt and two cardigans.

the sickly *city slicker*

A friend who works in the City told me about a colleague of his who's a real yuppie commuter.

He'd been out after work, celebrating heavily in a wine bar all night, and as usual had to run to catch the last train home. He was there in his double-breasted pin-stripe suit and light trench coat with his portable phone and Filofax safely in his leather briefcase. The train was packed with late revellers and other office workers going home and the swaying and lurching of the ancient rolling stock was making him feel more than a bit queasy. There was a sudden jolt and he knew he was going to throw up, so he opened the briefcase and nearly filled it to the brim.

The next day he woke up with an appalling hangover, remembering with a shudder about his case and that his wife was downstairs making his sandwiches. He leapt out of bed, ran downstairs and burst into the kitchen just in time to see his wife picking up his case.

'Don't open that!' he blurted out.

'Why?' she asked, ignoring him and opening it, only to find it was completely empty. Someone else's wife must have got a nasty shock that morning . . .

the night *stalker*

A friend of my dad's always drank in the same boozer down a leafy country lane, and was in the habit of taking a piece of meat with him in his pocket.

Every night he'd stagger out of the bar, slightly the worse for wear, take out the morsel of meat and hold it above his head. An owl that roosted nearby would swoop silently down, snatch the meat and fly off to a tree to eat it, every time.

One night he left the pub after a particularly heavy session and had an overwhelming urge to relieve himself there and then, so he staggered over to a suitable bush and did so. Obviously confused, the ravenous owl swooped down, talons poised, for its usual portion of flesh . . .

> Which just goes to show it's not always the early bird that catches the, er, worm.

chinese *poodle*

A wealthy husband and wife went out for a meal at a busy new local Chinese restaurant, taking their pet poodle with them.

During the meal, their pampered pooch kept whining, so the woman beckoned to one of the waiters, who came over to her. She asked if it might be possible for him to find something for her dog to eat so he didn't feel left out.

The waiter obviously didn't understand her, so she said the same again, only louder and slower. He shook his head and grunted.

So the woman, who had spent some time travelling round the Empire when Britain had one, set about explaining her wish using hand gestures, pointing to the poodle, then her plate and then her stomach, and making 'yum yum' sounds.

The waiter's face lit up and he indicated he understood. So he leant forward and took the dog's lead from the woman's hand and led the frisky poodle away.

Twenty minutes later, the waiter returned the poodle to the couple's table. Though to their horror, it was now roasted on a silver plate with an orange in its mouth and all the trimmings.

> This myth is often told with more than a hint of racism about the local Chinese or Indian restaurant, and plays on the Anglo-Saxon's deep-seated fear of anything foreign, especially 'spicy' food. Variations on the theme include:
>
> 'The local Chinese near us was raided by the police and environmental health, and they closed

it down because in the freezer they found half-eaten Alsatians hanging up and cats' carcasses in the waste skips . . .'

Which is often followed by, 'Well, they eat dogs in China don't they', 'they eat Derby winners for dinner in France', and 'the Italians make pies out of our migrating songbirds', or the evergreen:

'You know in Hong Kong they have special tables with holes in that close round a monkey's head, and they chop the top off its skull and eat its brains . . .'

Then there's the rejoinder, 'Well, if it tastes OK, I'm not complaining.' It's the *knowing* that's nasty, and always has been, ever since Sweeney Todd introduced his new line in pies. Talking of mystery ingredients . . .

southern-fried *rodent*

A friend had gone to the local fleapit to see the latest all-American Hollywood blockbuster. Feeling a bit peckish, she dashed into a well-known fast food outlet and bought a carton of southern American-style fried chicken and took it into the cinema.

As she was a bit late the lights were already down when she settled herself at the back. The movie began and she started to tuck into her grub, munching her way through the entire film.

When the lights came up she looked down into the carton and saw, to her horror, the back leg and tail of what was unmistakably a large fried rat.

an offal *experience*

A friend's mother had left it a bit late to sort out the family's evening meal, and not having anything to hand, she dashed down to the local butcher's.

To her concern, they'd sold everything apart from some dodgy-looking liver that was definitely on the turn, but they said she could have it cheap, so she took it. She put her bargain in the fridge and went about her chores.

A few hours later she opened the fridge to start the tea and to her horror, the 'liver' had crawled up the side of a milk bottle.

nowt *taken out*

A Yorkshire family was sitting down to tea and slicing up the bread for chip butties. Father cut a slice that seemed to have a small black mark in the centre. The mark got bigger with each slice, until the stunned family could gradually make out the shape of a dead mouse baked into the loaf.

keep it under *your hat*

Before the fall of Communism in the old Soviet Union food was often in short supply, especially meat products – unlike today.

In a supermarket in Moscow, a woman, who had been standing for hours in a typically lengthy checkout queue, collapsed. The concerned staff rushed to loosen her clothing and discovered that she had been trying to steal a frozen chicken, by smuggling it out under her large fur hat.

In a peculiar twist of fate, the pilfered poultry had frozen her brain solid and she was quite dead.

pea*nut*

A health visitor my brother knows used to regularly visit an old geezer in Edmonton, north London. Every time she went round, he'd fix up something for her to eat: cake and biscuits, or sandwiches. He so looked forward to her visits.

One day, he was a little ill, so she popped round to see him unannounced. He was very pleased to see her, but was flustered because he had no food to offer her apart from a little bag with a few peanuts in it.

She picked out a handful and munched on them. The old fellow told her to finish them, so she ate another load.

'I can't eat the peanuts anyway, they get stuck in my falsies,' he explained, adding, 'I just suck the chocolate off them.'

> Shades of Will Hay, Moore Marriott and a bag of boiled sweets about that one: Hay takes a red one, and old man Marriott says, 'D'you like the red ones? I always spit 'em out and put them back in the packet.'

fruity *salad*

The Mambo Inn, a club in Brixton, London, famous for its tropical music and cosmopolitan crowd, was treated to a spectacle one night. A macho Latin-American type was creating a bit of a stir on the dancefloor, as much for the inviting bulge in his tight leather trousers as his luscious lambada steps. But after about an hour of sensual movement, the sweat-soaked demon dancer suddenly fainted and collapsed in the middle of the dancefloor, to gasps. Luckily a doctor was at hand, and he was soon aware that the problem was a serious obstacle to the victim's blood circulation. There were more gasps when the doctor undid the man's flies, reached in and . . . pulled out a huge cucumber that had stopped the blood flow in the man's thighs. Cucumber Man was never seen at the Mambo again.

one *lump or two?*

A deeply religious mother of seven in rural Killarney had nagged her workshy husband into redecorating the entire house in honour of the 'Stations of the Cross' ceremony.

The exterior of the small terrace was freshly painted and the inside spring-cleaned with a vengeance.

The woman decided to top it all off by asking the local priest round to afternoon tea. The venerable cleric was happy to fit the date into his busy schedule and looked forward to the Sunday afternoon, as the woman was a renowned cook and a generous host.

When the day dawned everything was in order: best china, lace tablecloth and a choice of three different fancy cakes all laid out with a vase of flowers in the front parlour.

Sadly it was a rainy day and all the kids were playing merry hell in the house. Worst of all they kept running into the front room and pinching the sugar lumps from the tea set.

The mother collared the youngest, giving him a firm clip round the ear and snatching the half empty sugar bowl

from his sticky grip, only then discovering to her horror it had been smashed in two.

It was just at that point the doorbell rang. More than a little flustered, the woman quickly picked up the sugar lumps, and to keep them out of harm's way stuffed them into her ample cleavage. The smiling priest commented on how nice the house was looking and, nibbling a slice of Madeira, made all the right noises about her proficiency in the kitchen. Then as she poured his tea, not spotting a sugar bowl, the priest asked, 'Do you have any sugar?'

Without thinking the woman fished a few lumps out of her cleavage. Then she innocently asked, 'Milk, Father?'

'No, No!' exclaimed the priest, leaping to his feet . . .

you *must be choking*

An old friend of my auntie who works as a hospital cleaner was flicking his mop around casualty when a man was hurriedly stretchered in clutching his throat and coughing violently. The curtains were pulled and a junior doctor dashed breathlessly to the bedside, but there was just enough of a gap for the orderly to eavesdrop and catch a glimpse of what occurred.

The doctor carefully opened the man's mouth, manipulated his forceps, and removed a tightly wedged obstruction. Then he examined it closely as the patient recovered with an antiseptic gargle.

'What were you eating when you started to choke?' asked the doctor.

The patient croaked that he'd been enjoying a portion of southern-fried chicken.

'Well, well,' continued the medic – whose brother was of course a vet – 'unless I'm very much mistaken, I've just removed a cat's collarbone from your windpipe.'

> The cat's bone choker story follows a perennially common theme, and should really be told with a multiple-choice facility – choose from 'southern-fried chicken', the 'local Malaysian', the 'new Thai pub-cafe' – with an instruction to delete according to prejudice.

gums *and plums*

A young woman from Northampton, excited about some new imported Chinese bubble gum boasting an everlasting chew, found to her delight that you could masticate for hours and still have something substantial in your mouth.

Her health-conscious parents had always warned her against swallowing, because as we all know, ingesting chewing gum gives you worms, so when her jaw got too achy, she spat the gum out into the foil it came in.

But looking down she was horrified to see the gum had a recognisable shape to it, and one that she was familiar with: apparently each piece of the everlasting gum contained a condom.

a sour *note*

A friend of a friend from East Anglia once knew a real skinflint who used to drink in the same local. The cheapskate always arrived at half past eight, regular as clockwork, ordered his pint of bitter, perched on his favourite stool, and saw out the rest of the evening without further troubling the bar staff. Such behaviour not only irritated the landlord, a batey fellow at the best of times, but also got the goat of the other regulars, especially as the parsimonious bloke was so smug about his thriftiness and immune to any ribbing.

There was only one way the others in the local could get back at the miserly imbiber. When he slipped off his stool to visit the toilet, one of the other drinkers would nip over and enjoy a large gulp of his warm beer. When the bloke came back from the urinal, he would explode to see his carefully nursed pint depleted in his absence, and harangue the whole bar, shouting and stabbing his finger, 'Who's bin at my pint? It were you, weren't it!'

Apparently this had gone on for some months, when one night the penny-pincher came up with an answer to deter any would-be surreptitious slurpers. When he went to the toilet, he stuck a little note by his pint, which said: 'I've spit in this!' But when he returned from his micturition he found his note slightly amended; next to 'I've spit in this!', some anonymous rogue had scrawled 'So have I!'

the *prime cut*

A friend of a friend, a West Country campsite owner-cum-gentleman farmer, was wending his way down the narrow country lanes one dark and stormy night towards his little patch of olde England ('Caravans welcome. No bikers. No travellers.')

Normally, he strictly obeyed the unwritten rules of rural motoring, i.e. hurtled down the snaking road at breakneck speed taking the corners on the wrong side of the road and blasting his horn at any stray animals that got in the way. But this particular night there was a large white refrigerated lorry clogging up the road – a red rag to a bull. The truck was rattling along at a hell of a lick, but the impatient bloke driving along behind it was fuming and weaving around looking for a passing place. Just then the lorry clattered over a pot-hole. The back door flew open and a solid muslin sack bounced out on to the road. The bloke slammed on the anchors, skidded to a halt and snatched up the cold package; it was too good an opportunity to miss. Through the drizzly headlights he saw the chunky bag was marked 'Lamb' and happily tossed it in the car, drooling all the way home at the bonus of a roast for supper.

He handed his surprised wife the package on his way through to the telly but was alarmed by a scream and loud thud as the poor woman collapsed.

It was soon clear why. In the cold light of the kitchen, the bloke realised that the sack was actually marked 'Limb' – it apparently contained an amputated leg originally *en route* from hospital to incinerator.

slap *happy*

A retired seafarer, who was known to an habitual ale-swilling acquaintance, always frequented the same pub in Cleethorpes and regularly met up with a motley crew of his old shipmates to swap tales, drink to excess and generally have a good crack.

The poor seaman had been deaf in one ear for as long as he could remember and always took up the end pew to get his good ear in pole position so his cronies couldn't make any jokes at his expense. One evening one of the crusty old salts was spinning a rip-roaring yarn punctuated with saucy hilarity, causing the deaf codger to guffaw just as he was taking a sup from his mild.

The belly laugh became a violent coughing fit. Luckily, one sharp-thinking ancient mariner sprang up and gave him a stout wallop on the back. Something torpedoed out of the old seadog's bad ear and on to the table: it was a corporation bus ticket, issued in 1940. And to the salt's glee, its removal restored his quota of good ears to the usual complement.

The old bloke was apparently so overjoyed at the restoration of his faculties that he splashed out on a round for everyone in the alehouse – all three of them.

the fist *anniversary*

A trawlerman's wife, who works out at the same aerobics class as a friend of our Beryl, was being taken out to celebrate her first wedding anniversary by her windswept husband. She was dressed up to the tens (that smart!) and he tugged on his best Arran jumper for an evening drenched in romance at the local Chinese.

For a change they didn't order a set meal for two but, carried away by the occasion, plunged headlong into the *à la carte* selections. Lambrusco chilling on ice, they tucked into the first course; a selection of sweet and sour – much like their topsy-turvy marriage, really.

Suddenly the woman began to choke and coughed up a small, half-chewed bone into her napkin. Then she blew her nose as a diversionary device and popped the napkin into her pocket without another thought.

The rest of the meal was marvellous, rounded off by her favourite treat, a mountain of banana fritters smothered in syrup. The bill wasn't too steep either and as they meandered back arm-in-arm, hubby suggested a night cap at the local.

Snuggled up in the corner, the bloke tucked into his lager top and his happy spouse sipped her Bailey's. They'd happened to find a table next to a bunch of old doctors from the locality celebrating a win on the horses.

Suddenly the woman felt a sneeze coming on and whipped out her napkin. The bone from the meal tumbled out and rolled across the table, coming to rest against one of the old medics' leather elbow patches.

The assembled doctors went very quiet and one of them

picked up the bone and examined it closely. He spoke very slowly.

'What a peculiar thing to carry around. Where did you get this?' he asked gravely.

The woman explained.

'Oh dear,' continued the venerable quack. 'Unless I'm very much mistaken, I think you'll find that it's a metacarpal – a human knuckle to you, madam!'

bottoms *up*

A Surreyman from Yorkshire lived in New Zealand back in the 1970s and gained some fascinating insights into the interdependency of the indigenous Maoris and more recent arrivals.

One wily old native New Zealander who lived on the outskirts of Nelson had a large family to feed and very little to do it with, so he had to rely on his wits. Luckily there was enough in that department to sustain an army.

The picturesque centrepiece of the municipality of Nelson is a large ornamental pond which is home to a wide and colourful variety of wildfowl. As students of economics will know, what we have here is an obvious case of supply and demand. Sadly, as in many commercial situations, there were problems, i.e. how to supply the ducks to his demanding family without attracting the attention of the authorities and leading them to interfere in the free function of his moral obligations. Luckily these problems were overcome with impressive enterprise.

Apparently the breadwinner had some metal rat traps welded up to his own specifications which he would load with cheese. These he would place in the shallows of the pond late at night. Then he'd return at first light before the pond authorities or general public could poke their noses in and harvest the ducks, bobbing with their bottoms up.

In this manner he could feed his entire family at surprisingly little cost to himself.

mythellaneous

Consumption

✱ There's a restaurant in Japan where, provided you pay the price, you can smash up all the crockery

✱ There's an eccentric pub in Hertfordshire that selects its own weird opening hours, and charges anything from a halfpenny 'in the old money' to £50 for two pints

✱ There are liqueur-style chocolates on sale in Amsterdam that have human blood in the liquid centre

✱ Other fondant selections on sale around the world include chocolates from Egypt with beetles inside and a French alternative, small dried frogs (of course)

✱ When Newcastle's Peter Beardsley was first called up for England, he nipped to a nearby Rowntree's factory and bought a tray of ha'penny chocolate misshapes to take down with him as a treat. 'Ee, the lads'll love these,' he said, inaccurately

✱ If you leave a tooth in a cup of fizzy cola overnight, it completely dissolves. As does a penny piece left in tomato sauce for long enough

✱ If you don't have one of the colours in your Smarties packet, write off and complain – they'll send you a load in the post

✱ Beware the chicken burger – that luxury 'mayonnaise' may turn out to be a cyst on the fowl

man's *best friends*

A menagerie of animal crackers

Poor dumb animals frequently fall foul of the most dangerous animals of them all – humans – and their rancid imaginations. For some reason they bring out the beast in us; on the other hand the whole who's zoo of creation seems intent on biting the hand that feeds it . . .

taking *the mickey*

My mum's neighbour's son bought a male pup and was as proud as punch of the little blighter. It grew into a strapping mongrel that would hold its own in any scrap on the estate, so the bloke was even more proud of its enviable reputation among his friends.

But one thing about the dog was a source of ridicule: when it went for a leak, it wouldn't cock its leg like a male dog, it would crouch down like a female. Local people were remorseless in their whooping laughter whenever the dog performed its wimpy act.

Eventually the owner was driven to distraction and could stand it no more. So he took his dog to the vet and asked his confidential advice. The vet packed him straight off to a top animal physiologist who'd come across this problem many times before and suggested there was a simple solution. 'The best thing to do is be a role model when you're out walking. Demonstrate to him yourself what he should be doing.'

For three weeks the barracking from his neighbours was infinitely worse, seeing him out with his dog and pretending to urinate against trees and lampposts.

But three weeks later, the dog had stopped crouching to leave a splash. One evening, the vet happened to pass as the owner and his dog were out 'walkies'. The animal doctor enquired how things had gone. 'See for yourself,' said the bloke, proudly indicating his pooch. The dog was having a leak all right, but standing upright on its hind legs in front of a tree, its front paws on its groin, and attempting to whistle – just like its owner.

the dead *rabbit*

My brother-in-law knows a cockney bloke who made his pile and moved his family out to the sticks, a really posh rustic village.

They weren't very popular in the new area because they were always banging car doors late at night, and they had one of those hyperactive dogs that's always yapping, chasing cyclists and catching things in nearby fields.

One day, though, the slavering hound came in with a

rabbit between its teeth. Not just any rabbit, this was obviously a domestic bunny – and next-door's at that. The kid would be mortified at the fate of his cherished pet, and his mum was always going on about the tone of the neighbourhood going right down.

The cockney racked his brain for a solution. Luckily the dog hadn't chewed up the rabbit, only made it dirty by playing with it; it must have died of shock. He took the furry fatality and cleaned it up, shampooing and even carefully blow-drying it. Then he quickly checked no one was in next door, before hopping over the fence and nestling the rabbit back in the straw bedding of its hutch.

Later at the weekend, he was out in the garden drinking a can of lager, when he saw his next-door neighbour. This was the conversation he'd been dreading . . .

She said that little Jimmy was very, very upset. 'It's about the rabbit,' she said, as the bloke felt increasingly uncomfortable.

'I only buried it on Wednesday, but it was back in the hutch on Friday.'

sex with *Nanny*

According to a lawyer we know, in a court in North Wales in the 1970s, a woman was apparently suing her husband for divorce, on the grounds that the marriage had never been consummated. The only problem was, she was heavily pregnant at the time.

Smirking, the judge gently suggested her condition might have quite a large bearing on the case; either the marriage nuptials had taken place, or the woman had been unfaithful. The woman denied both. Sheepishly, she sincerely explained that she'd been having a sexual relationship with a ghost. The judge kept a straight face and turned to the courtroom, asking if anyone else had ever had sex with a ghost. To his surprise, a ruddy-faced old farmer-type at the back looked around and timidly raised his hand.

Incredulously, the judge bellowed, 'You've really had sex with a ghost?'

'Oh,' said the old fellow, blanching, 'I thought you said "goat".'

monkey-hanging *business*

A classic English myth concerns the people of Hartlepool on the north-east coast, an allegedly simple folk and even simpler in the time of the story, which took place during the Napoleonic wars at the beginning of the nineteenth century.

Apparently, a fleet of French ships was sighted in the North Sea and harried by English vessels until they were virtually obliterated. But one of Boney's boats was seen sailing just off the coast of Hartlepool, and local braves were sent out to apprehend it for king and country.

This they did with little difficulty, for the crew was entirely absent save for a little monkey dressed in a tiny uniform of Napoleon's navy. Never having seen a Frenchman before, and with no one to compare him with, the good populace of Hartlepool arrested him as an enemy sailor. The monkey was then tried, pronounced guilty and hanged. And with no character witnesses . . .

This story is still the source of some discomfort to Hartlepudlians. Mindful of the potential for mischief, local lads from neighbouring towns (Sunderland, Newcastle, Middlesbrough) occasionally dress up in monkey costumes and go on pub crawls around Hartlepool – to be followed around by bad-tempered youths with a score to settle.

Another angle lies in the spread of this myth. There are Kent people who swear the monkey-hanging townsfolk were natives of their country – all other details remaining the same. If you know of any other places that should be twinned with Hartlepool for their animal activities, the authors would love to hear about them.

For the record, there's a theme pub on Cleveland Street, London W1, that displays the whole sorry story.

paws for *thought*

An English family were sightseeing in the famous American nature reserve Yellowstone Park in a hired station wagon, and stopped abruptly when they found themselves surrounded by a posse of large bears.

After a while they determined to proceed slowly through them, making sure windows were wound up. As they moved off, they found one bear was following them close behind and howling aggressively. They sped up a little, but the howling bear just trotted faster, keeping right behind them.

Eventually, the car was travelling so speedily that the exhausted bear fell over and lay down in the road growling in a high-pitched fashion. When they arrived back at their hotel, they went to the trunk to remove their picnic things and noticed, to their eternal shame, a patch of bloody fur and two of the unfortunate bear's claws, jammed behind the wagon's sharp chrome bumper.

uncool for *cats*

My uncle used to be a long distance lorry driver, and a mate of his on the Manchester to Glasgow run had a rather nasty experience.

One cold winter's night the rain was bucketing down, and the lorry driver had his headlights and wipers full on just to be able to see enough to carry on. He'd had a flat tyre earlier in the day and was driving on late through the atrocious conditions in a vain attempt to make up time. Peering out of the steamed-up windscreen, white knuckles clutching the steering wheel, his headlights suddenly picked out a startled cat frozen with fear in the middle of the road.

He slammed on the anchors, the lorry skidded, and there was a horrible bump.

Now the lorry driver was a cat lover himself, and feeling sickeningly guilty, leapt from his cab to find the stricken animal. It was writhing in agony on the roadside verge, so he did the decent thing: took out his shovel and put it out of its misery.

After that nasty turn, the driver continued on his way but pulled over at the next pub to steady his nerves. He'd just begun to calm down with a half of bitter, when a policeman entered the inn and arrested him. A tearful old lady had just rung them.

It appears she'd popped out to call her beloved moggy in from the appalling weather and had seen the lorry run over next-door's cat. Her own feline had been playing around in some long grass by the side of the road, when the lorry driver had pulled up, got out and despatched it with his spade.

yucky *Yucca*

A work colleague told me about her friend who had a nasty experience with an exotic parlour palm. She'd been out shopping in everyone's mum's favourite store, famous for its reliability and underwear, and purchased a Yucca plant. It was a fine specimen and immediately it took pride of place in the living-room, and was looked after with extra special care.

It was while watering the parlour palm that she noticed an ominous clicking noise coming from the plant. At first she thought nothing of it, but it nagged away at her and at each watering the sound seemed to get worse. So she called up the store to complain.

The person who answered the phone was most anxious. She told the woman to stay exactly where she was, not to touch the plant or go near it, and said there would be someone straight round.

A few minutes later there was a knock on the door and four men in head-to-toe protective clothing, looking like something out of *Aliens*, came into the living-room and spread out a large rubber sheet. They put the Yucca in the middle of the sheet and carefully lifted it out of its pots . . . to reveal a large mother tarantula with hundreds of babies crouched in the black fur of her back.

That's another hardy perennial tabloid-style

myth. In fact, in April 1992 (not the 1st!), a London radio news broadcast resurrected the old chestnut of a trader at Spitalfields market being bitten by a spider that came out of a bunch of bananas shipped in from Colombia. As usual, though, there was no name, no interview . . . no proof.

dirty *dog*

A politician at the last general election was canvassing his large constituency and came to a terraced house with a slavering pit bull outside. He hated dogs, and was a bit hesitant as he pressed the doorbell, but he was given a warm welcome by the people of the house.

They told him they always voted for him anyway, and pleased to meet him, invited him in for a cup of tea. He was feeling pretty parched after a tough morning's door-stepping and accepted their offer, edging past the growling pit bull.

The dog followed him to heel into the room and lay down showing its teeth and staring at him from the middle of the floor.

He was enjoying his cup of tea as much as he could with the dog there, chatting with his constituents about local issues, when the dog stood up, cocked its leg and completely soaked the carpet. His hosts looked at the dog briefly, then carried on talking.

The politician was a bit taken aback, but as no one else said anything, he just wondered a bit about what kind of supporter he was attracting. Each to their own, he decided.

After a good chinwag, the candidate drained his cup,

thanked the family, and made his way out of the door. He'd just taken a few paces outside when he heard someone call out behind him:

'Excuse me, aren't you going to take your dog with you?'

bacon *lined*

My grandad told me that when he was a lad, he and his mates used to play a cunning trick on the feathered residents of a large pond near where they lived in Droylsden, Manchester.

The lads would go up to the pond, take a length of string and tie a piece of fatty bacon rind to it. The hungry, unsuspecting ducks would swim over thinking they were in for a treat. The lads would throw the bacon rind to the first duck who'd snaffle it up immediately.

Now it's a little known fact that bacon rind goes through a duck much like a string through a goose (makes sense) – or even a dose of salts, whichever is the quickest. Anyway, the rind passed straight through the duck and floated on the water, and the next starving duck gobbled it up. The same thing happened again and again until there was a long line of ducks all connected by a piece of string.

The lads would lead them around for a while, then take one duck and start pulling its leg just like I'm pulling yours.

> We're not totally sure about biological accuracy relating to the speed of a duck's digestive system, or whether one duck would fancy eating something which had so recently passed through another duck. All we can say is please don't try this at home.

posing *pouch*

The crew from a British magazine were going on a fashion shoot in the Australian outback, and were driving along an empty dirt road in their Shogun 4 × 4, when from nowhere a kangaroo suddenly bounded into their path, and they hit it full on.

They all jumped out to see if it was OK, but it had quite obviously died of shock. The tasteless art director of the shoot decided it would be a great gimmick to make use of the poor creature and lobbed the carcass in the boot.

Then, when they arrived at their location, he dressed the kangaroo up in some of the expensive designer clobber the models were supposed to wear, and propped it up to take the snaps.

But in the blink of a shutter, the kangaroo recovered from its concussion, stood up and bounded off into the bush, still wearing the glamorous creations of Jean-Paul Gaultier, Yohji Yamomoto and Mr Byrite.

the dead *budgie*

A friend's gran called in some plumbers to fix a dodgy old gas fire in her house in Aberdeen. The blokes turned up on the allotted day and set to fixing the fire. Gran decided to pop out down the shops while they were on the job, and did so.

The gas-fitters were a right couple of cowboys. They kept on dropping the monkey wrench and smashing tiles on the fireplace, and there were bits of the fire all over the shop. What's more, the gas fire was leaking like a sieve while they were messing about. Eventually, though, they

107

got it back together with only a few nuts and washers left over at the end.

As they stood up to have a fag, one of them noticed that the budgie had fallen off its perch and was lying on the floor of its cage with its little legs in the air — stone dead. Realising there'd be hell to pay when the old lady came home and saw they'd gassed her pet, the two bodgers took some copper wire and fastened the deceased bird upright on his perch. Then they cleared up, and were ready to be off when they heard the keys in the door.

The old lady came into the living-room, took one look at the budgie's cage and fainted.

When they'd revived her, she explained that she had been deeply shocked to see the budgie on its perch again — as it had died earlier that morning.

horse *shoot*

A friend of a friend from Jersey was going rabbit shooting with his mate up in the hills. They planned to check out a place where they'd never shot before that was riddled with rabbit holes, and where you'd often see the furry vermin hopping about their hillside warren.

Most farmers were only too pleased to let the blokes blast their rabbit problem to kingdom come, but the hunters thought it only good manners to ask permission first. They turned up at the farm early one morning and one of them went down to the farmhouse to see the landowner.

The farmer was very hospitable, offering the stranger a steaming mug of strong tea and a hunk of bread and jam. He happily gave the blokes the run of his estate to dispatch as many rabbits as possible. They were a terrible nuisance, forever eating his crops and burrowing under his fences.

Eyeing the gun, the farmer then asked the bloke if he could beg a favour in return.

'There's an old horse up in the top field that's really suffering. I've been meaning to get rid of him, but the knackers want *me* to pay *them* to turn him into dog meat. So perhaps you wouldn't mind shooting him and I'll clear up later,' he said.

Agreeable to shooting anything, the hunter trudged back up the path to his chum. Then a wicked thought occurred to him, and he decided to play a trick on his trigger-happy companion.

They set off together up the hill and when he was out of range of the farmhouse the bloke started swearing about how obnoxious the farmer had been, shouting at him to 'Get orff my larnd!' and prodding his rear with a pitchfork. Just as they reached the top field, the bloke really laid it on thick. 'That old farmer's really got my goat!' he yelled. 'No one speaks to me like that!' And he lifted his blaster shoulder high and shot the farmer's old horse dead to impress his mate.

But he'd miscalculated his friend's solidarity. Picking up his own shooter, the other bloke yelled, 'Yer, too right,' and promptly slaughtered two cows.

While the above story takes place in the countryside, it illustrates only too well city dwellers' well-supported belief that country folk really hate animals. Urbanites like to believe that the animals on our farmyards all have names like Dobbin, Daisy and Clarabel and live a life of Old Mac-

Donald rural bliss. Whereas real country dwellers prefer to see them as new McDonalds and money in the bank. Nowadays Daisy's really called E239875432KZ and she's on more drugs than a Bulgarian weightlifter. Even our indigenous wildlife is under threat from the homicidal yokels. I mean, how many city folk go charging around in a bloodthirsty posse, dressed to kill, with a pack of mad dogs chasing a tiny little terrified adversary – Millwall fans apart?

messy *moggy*

A haulage firm based near King's Lynn used to allow a number of feral cats on site in order to keep the problem of vermin under control. But casualties were frequent; the cats would take shelter anywhere around the artics – on the wheels, on the axles, under the cab – and never seemed to learn. So the company sealed an arrangement with a local vet so that any cat injured could be taken, any time, day or night, to the surgery for treatment.

The scheme proved successful, and in return for a number of recuperating felines, the boss of the company would drop round the odd treat off the back of one of his lorries.

Then one morning the haulage guv'nor got a furious call from the vet. Ear still burning, he called his drivers in to explain. After a minute one stepped forward.

'Well, boss,' he said, 'I ran over a cat in me lorry, right, and I went down the vet's. But it was closed, so I slipped the cat under the door with a note.'

An American version of these 'stupid things to do with a dead cat'-type stories has a couple renting a house in a neighbourhood, then going on a touring holiday for three weeks. After a few days they notice a dead cat in the back of their car – they've got a sun-roof and reckon it must've fallen in from a tree-branch. They recognise the cat as their neighbours', and keep it in a bag. At the end of their holiday, they return home to find the neighbours are now on holiday, so they thoughtfully deposit the moggy in its owners' postbox and keep schtum.

ruff guide *to Spain*

One of my gran's old pals from chorus-line music-hall days was on holiday with a bunch of senior citizens in Benidorm.

The old dear loved animals, and every morning she would take a few scraps out to the compound gates and feed the local strays on the beach. There were scrawny Spanish pooches of all shapes, all typically tiny, and being a soft-hearted old girl, she immediately fell for the skinniest little wretch of the bunch, and cossetted it most of all.

When the holiday drew to a close the old dear couldn't bear to leave her scruffy little chum to the hard life of the streets, and ignoring the stringent quarantine regulations and the danger of rabies, she resolved to smuggle the toy dog back to Blighty.

With the diversionary tactics of a few of the other senior citizens, involving a dodgy pacemaker and some Winter-green's ointment, she breezed through customs and got her

little pal home in a jiffy. Letting her new pet out of his parcel, the old lady introduced him to her cat.

The tom took one look and attacked. A terrible fight ensued. Plants went flying, curtains were ruined and an umbrella stand spilled over.

The old dear finally broke them up and there was blood everywhere. She rushed the poor little Spanish dog straight to the vet's. The animal doctor took one look and asked her what she thought it was.

'What can you mean? It's a dog,' said the elderly dame.

'I've got news for you,' said the vet sternly. 'This, madam, is a giant gutter rat.'

The kind-hearted lady and her cherished rat-dog

formed the title story of Jan Harold Brunvand's collection of American apocryphal stories *The Mexican Pet*, and is one of those that appears rooted in the observation of the sorry condition of some Spanish/Mexican breeds, and the misplaced sympathy of those who ignore the threat of rabies. Who'd be a chihuahua, though? The diminutive dogs are all too often the butt of mythical accidents: frequently sat upon and killed or attacked by big domestic cats who think they are rats. Read on . . .

cat *in the bag*

Driving home from work one day, a friend of my aunt's who lives in a less than salubrious area ran over her pet cat.

She was very upset at the moggy's demise, but being a practical woman immediately set about clearing up the unfortunate animal in preparation for a decent burial. So she popped the squashed beast into a handy green Marks and Spencer's bag, then opened the boot to get her shopping.

Just as she battled with too much shopping, a scruffy woman rushed up and snatched the M&S bag with the dead cat in it and scarpered around the corner.

Seconds later, there was a squeal of brakes and a sickening thud. Aunt's friend dropped her shopping and dashed to see what had happened. There lying crumpled on the ground surrounded by a group of people was the bag-snatcher.

An ambulance was called and the woman stretchered inside. The paramedics were just closing the rear door when someone piped up, 'Here, don't forget this – she was looking at that when she got hit.'

And he popped the M&S bag inside the ambulance.

feather *light*

It was those hazy crazy lazy days of summer again, and a mate was looking after his nan's budgerigar while she kept her Wednesday afternoon appointment at the hairdresser's for a shampoo and set.

The little feathered chap was looking a bit down in the beak, so the lad let it out of its cage to stretch its wings.

Like a blue thunderbolt the grass parakeet shot out of his hand and smashed straight into the window. Clearly

quite dazed and confused, the ruffled fancy bird was limping forlornly in circles on the kitchen lino.

Its leg was obviously very painful, and possibly broken. Reckoning a little first aid was in order, the resourceful lad took some cotton and tied a matchstick to the injured budgie's limb to act as a splint, before popping him back behind bars. The peg-leg hopped across the bottom of his cage towards his cuttlefish. Then, inevitably, the match ignited on the sandpaper sheet, the flames spreading quickly to his feathers and barbecuing the poor bird.

walk*ies!*

An elderly woman who used to be the doctor's receptionist at my uncle's surgery lived in a quiet part of Harrogate. In her comfortable retirement, the dotty woman – a widow – had found a furry companion with whom to share the autumn of her life. It was a gorgeous little poodle and she was devoted to it, cladding it in ribbons and other canine accoutrements.

The spoilt pooch went everywhere with its venerable owner, and was as pampered as Mrs Slocombe's pussy. She wouldn't let it out in wind or moderate sunshine, and at the first sign of rain or a sniffy-nosed dog, she would rush home to save her mutt from a cold or worse. When she was on heat, the poor bitch was locked inside for days.

But one day, as the sun was shining brightly and there wasn't a dog to be seen anywhere around, the myopic woman drove over to a nice park in her old Morris Minor. It had been raining for days and she'd promised her pet a good runaround.

After a lovely stroll round the municipal fields, the old

dame was just returning to her car when a friend tapped her on the shoulder. They hadn't seen each other for years and there was a lot to catch up on, what with deaths to go over, infidelities to dissect, new hats to pour scorn on and so forth. The poor poodle got frustrated and began tugging on its lead. The woman was being pulled all over the place and the lead was getting under her feet, so she temporarily tied the leash to the back bumper of her car and continued her chinwag in peace. It was a toasty summer day, and she always heeded the RSPCA's advice about not leaving dogs in cars on hot days in case they dehydrated.

After a few minutes the poodle was getting very agitated, but for once the woman ignored her pride and joy. Then it began yelping loudly; oddly though, the whine seemed to drift away. Naturally concerned, the old dear broke off the chat to check things were OK. To her horror, she saw her beloved pooch being dragged along the tarmac by an accelerating car. The soppy dame had attached the leash to the wrong car's bumper.

horse *play*

Horses don't have much of a life when it comes down to it, especially the racing ones: from punter's fancy to steak pie in the snap of a fetlock. But there was one poor old nag whose fate was worse than Shergar's (far worse: the famous missing thoroughbred is apparently crunching carrots in Libya after a top-secret 'arms-for-bloodstock' deal).

The twelve-year-old horse, not the top racer in its Wiltshire stables, was lined up to race at a national hunt meeting a couple of hundred miles away. But its hard-hearted trainer had used up all his good boxes on mounts with a more realistic chance of success, so for the journey north it had to fit into a decrepit one-pony transporter salvaged from a haystack in a swampy part of the yard. The horse box looked like something a New Age traveller would keep his or her dog in rather than the conveyance for a classy hunk of horseflesh.

Warily, the horse staggered up the splintered gangplank and entered the dilapidated crate. It was awful: no windows, no space, no eating facilities, a decayed floor and the rancid smell of chicken wee – exactly like a student flat-share, in other words.

The sad old stallion was reassured by the callous trainer and locked in the dark as the Frontera towing it lurched off down the muddy lane.

If only the trainer had watched a little longer, he may have averted an utterly awful equine tragedy, for just a few hundred yards down the road the poor horse's hooves went through the rotten floor of the transporter. But despite the dreadful panicking whinny, the driver kept his heavy foot to the floor. By the time the transporter pulled to a halt, the nag's legs were sadly worn down to stumps.

the labrador *let-off*

A mate of my uncle's was working on his Ford Escort at the top of the hill in Ilford where he lived. In order to keep an eye on his Labrador dog, he'd locked it inside the car. He was working under the engine, when he heard a snarling sound, and then a mechanical clunk.

All of a sudden, the car rolled forwards, and he was just able to scramble out of the way. He couldn't believe his eyes when he saw that his dog had taken the handbrake off and was standing with its paws on the steering wheel, as if it was driving. He was so surprised in fact that he didn't move fast enough to open the door, and the Escort careered halfway down the hill and ended up demolishing a neighbour's privet hedge.

underhand *undercarriage*

A Liverpudlian chancer who a friend once met in a pub was dead proud of his new dog, a young pedigree Rottweiler that he hoped to enter for shows. Until, that is, a neighbour pointed out that the hound appeared to be lacking in the gonad department. The Scouser examined his pet between the legs and was mortified to discover that the bag was as empty as a soggy old balloon.

Clearly this put paid to his hopes of dog show glory and the lucrative breeding fees that could be commanded by a top dog. So the owner contacted his vet and had spherical silicon implants (extra large) fitted in his Rott's scrotum. Now fully equipped, the noble beast was entered for every prestige dog show around the country.

For a couple of months this fantastic example of canine manhood won everything in sight, and breeders queued up to have their prize bitches serviced. But before the first of these profitable ventures was tied up, the prize dog had another show to enter.

Victory seemed to be a foregone conclusion until one of the judges started taking an inordinate interest in the Rottweiler's toilet area. As the adjudicator fondled the dog's undercarriage, disaster struck. The poor mutt's original testicles dropped, plopping into the judge's cupped hand, and all its owner's plans fell flat.

red *or dead*

Some engaged friends of a woman at work were strolling through a leafy park in Glasgow, soaking up the early spring sunshine when something caught the woman's eye, and she gasped. For just up ahead of them was a red squirrel squashed flat on the path. There were precious few of these beautiful indigenous creatures left without this kind of tragedy. The couple dashed over to the animal and the woman, choking back the tears, stooped down to carry the motionless squirrel into the woods and at least afford it some final dignity in death.

But suddenly the prostrate squirrel's eyes flashed open fiendishly. Then the beast pounced, tore a large chunk out of the stunned woman's outstretched figure, and sprinted away up a tree.

The poor woman was still distraught as her beau bandaged a handkerchief round the wound and swiftly drove her to Casualty. The boyfriend comforted his love as best he could while they waited in the long queue. As her sobs subsided she got talking to a sweet old lady in the next seat.

After a few pleasantries the couple asked the woman why she was there – she looked as fit as a butcher's dog. 'Well,' the old dear began, raising a bandaged hand, 'I was walking through the park thus morning when I saw a poor wee red squirrel lying on the path . . . '

cat *eats dog*

A family in Durham entrusted their pampered pooch, a chihuahua, with friendly neighbours while they went to

119

Lourdes (or was it Lords?) for a few days. The neighbours were happy to oblige, though they were slightly concerned how their huge rag-eared ginger tom might react – that immense cat was a horrendous scrapper.

On the first day, the couple let their petite charge out into the garden to exercise its tiny legs. A few minutes later, they began to wonder if things were a bit too quiet and slipped out to have a look.

To their horror, the monster moggy was lying on the lawn prancing around with the half-eaten and obviously dead toy dog in its paws. The neighbours acted quickly, retrieving the carcass from the cat's claws and inventing a suitable story to steer the blame away from their pet.

When the people next door returned from their jaunt, the neighbours caught them before they went inside and explained in hushed tones that their dog had suddenly developed an horrific illness. They'd rushed it straight to the vet, who advised them that there was no hope: the poor thing was in such pain the only thing to do was put it out of its misery.

The sorrowful dog owners thanked their friends for their kindness and sloped back to their house. But an hour later, the bloke next door was back, and not in such a charitable mood.

'Are you sure our little dog was put down at the vet?' he asked, sternly. The couple nodded sheepishly.

'I only ask because I found this on our back door step.' And he held up the bloody, half-chewed head of his cherished chihuahua.

Over in the newly democratised former Soviet Union many new capitalist enterprises are battling for supremacy. The route to the top is obviously through trade, and what could be better than exchange with good old Uncle Sam, conqueror of Communism and guardian of world democracy (unless you happen to be Grenada, or Nicaragua, or anything to do with oil . . .)

One Russian businessman decided he'd steal a march on his competitors and arrange a prestigious bear hunt for his potential American trading partners to curry favour. America has murdered virtually all its own bears, so it's only fair we should let them clear up the last few elsewhere, too. Plus they don't care how much they pay to do it.

Risk management is top of the tree at Moscow MBA college these days and the wily Ruskie thought he'd completely remove the potential for failure from the hunt by purchasing an ancient toothless circus bear who loved people and couldn't even have given you a nasty suck if he'd tried. With every option covered the businessman started counting dollars in the bank; the 'canned hunt' couldn't fail to be a roaring success (without too much of the roaring).

The day of the hunt dawned. The affable old bruin was released into the woods and the excited American hunting party began stalking. After a couple of hours with their guns cocked they were closing in on the tired old panting animal. In fact they could see it with the naked eye, ambling along ahead in a clearing by the roadside.

Steeling themselves to dispatch the hirsute beast, the Yanks were astonished by an outlandish turn of events that wrecked their sport. A whistling peasant cycling to market happened to wobble round the corner, came face to face with the shaggy brute and fell off his velocipede.

Momentarily remembering his twenty years in the ring, the sprightly old bear leapt on the bicycle, wheeled around in a circle and pedalled off as fast as his paws would take him.

dressing *for dinner*

A Polish woman, short of a crust and on the breadline, was the toast of her family after at last scraping together enough cash to buy a chicken for the big Sunday dinner. It was the middle of winter and the faces of the under-nourished kids shone in the candlelight. Her husband licked his lips in anticipation as she lifted the old boiler out of the sack and rapidly set about plucking it. A pan of water and locally-gathered herbs was put on to boil up for a soup *hors d'oeuvre*.

All of a sudden, the family's slap-up hopes were dashed in the most shocking fashion. The poor woman had pretty much plucked the whole bird when, tugging the last few quills from what one presumes was a particularly sensitive area, the hen, obviously stunned rather than killed by the farmer, leapt from her hands squawking, feeling raw, sore, but very much alive, and began clucking round the poor family's kitchen. The woman was mortified; partly because her family looked like missing their long-awaited nosh, but mostly because she felt so guilty at defeathering the bird alive. They all agreed to liberate the bird, but the children were concerned it wouldn't last five minutes in the freezing cold without its downy insulation.

Thinking swiftly, the Polish matriarch asked her youngest child to hurry and find some baby clothes. Then while her husband held it still, she dressed the chicken in the 'hen-me-downs' from leg to breast (even a crocheted bonnet). Not exactly the dressing she'd planned for it in the oven, but . . .

Shortly afterwards the family gathered round as their mother took the fowl outside to the front of the house and tearfully set it free. The chicken appeared dazed at first and stood there in its babygrow and other clothes. Then it darted away, straight out into the nearby main road. As luck would have it, a motorist happened to be steaming round the bend and spotted the darting swaddling clothes. Convinced he was about to waste a toddler, the driver veered off the road at the last minute, storming through some bushes and coming to a halt embedded in the front wall of the poor woman who'd just liberated the chicken.

> So that's why the chicken crossed the road (groan). Another fowl story doing the rounds concerns one of our rarest and most beautiful birds.

caught *shorty*

An old dear who's a bingo partner of my gran had always had a hankering to see the Highlands of Scotland before she popped her clogs, and booked herself on a crumblies' coach tour of the glens.

As she never went anywhere without her faithful Yorkie, she popped him inside her souvenir shopping bag with his head sticking out – his usual mode of transport. The wee dog was fairly well behaved on the bus and was a big hit with the other old cronies who were forever feeding the little fellow titbits from their Tupperware.

They trundled around the sights of the Highlands for a couple of days – salmon farms, Highland dancing demonstrations, displays of heavy drinking and fighting, excursions to woollen shops and the like.

One day the tiny dog yapped as it did when it needed the use of a suitable bush. So the old lady followed the usual routine, called the coach to a halt, set the little fellow down and turned a blind eye. Sadly a golden eagle hovering above kept *its* eye peeled. It spotted the tasty morsel, swooped down and carried the yapping pooch off in its talons.

myth*ellaneous*

Nature

✽ Pigs are very good swimmers, but they daren't take the plunge for fear of their razor-sharp, thrashing trotters slitting their throats

✽ Robins have regional accents that they pick up from their relatives and friends

✽ Starlings can impersonate car alarms and switch them off

✽ One scene in the Bayeux Tapestry (1067) depicts a kangaroo (Australia was 'discovered' 700 years later). It's somewhere near panel 48

✽ Cuddly koalas are actually vicious – one once bit the Queen

✽ When a tiger's skin splits along its back, that beast will become a man-eater

✽ Sri Lankan elephant boys give their charges 'speed' to make them work just that little bit faster

✽ If a large vicious dog attacks you, the best way to avoid being savaged is to grab its front legs and swiftly yank them apart sideways, killing it instantly

✽ If a cow licks your bald pate, your hair grows back – but it has to be the right type of cow

✽ You can save a Spanish bull from certain death in the ring only by marrying it

✽ If you pick a hamster up by the tail, its eyes pop out

∗ A woman once lost her watch on a Devon beach. Years later, her husband caught a fish in the same spot and it had her watch inside – still keeping perfect time

occupational *hazards*

Nine-to-five nonsense

The workplace is a most fertile ground for myth production, and this little lot prove that most accidents don't happen in the home. Perhaps it's the fierceness of internal office politics, perhaps the nine-to-five tedium, or perhaps just the liquid lunches, that makes minds wander into the realms of vindictive fantasy. Health and safety take second place when there's a job to be done, especially an 'odd' one. The spirit of 'the long stand' lives on . . .

the deer-*stalker*

A friend of mine recalls a man at his office who was quite high-up but a pompous old buffer, and therefore unpopular with his workmates. One day, he was browsing in the local market and came across a Sherlock Holmes-style deer-stalker hat, which he bought and wore to work, to everyone's quiet amusement.

Unfortunately for him, a few days later, two of his colleagues chanced upon the same market stall, and decided to purchase two more identical titfers – one in the largest size available, the other the smallest.

The next day, he hung his 'stalker up in reception as usual. The two colleagues whipped it off its hook, replacing it with the large one they'd bought. At the end of the day, the old buffer picked up the hat and put it on, and was quite surprised to find that it was far too big, but he didn't think much about it and went home with the hat resting on his ears.

The next day, they replaced the largest hat with the smallest, which perched precariously on top of his cranium . . . and so they went on, day after day for weeks – sometimes leaving the bloke's original hat for a few days – until eventually the distraught old buffer paid a visit to his GP, convinced that his head was expanding and contracting like a balloon.

papier *man-mâché*

A friend who worked as a safety officer in a large Lancashire paper mill knew of a workmate who put himself about a bit. The mill took all sorts of paper waste – newspapers, cardboard packaging – and pulped it in massive vats with huge revolving blades at the bottom for recycling.

Every now and then, a load of girlie mags would arrive for pulping, though many would disappear before reaching the threshing blades. One day, just such a porn consignment arrived.

Now the vats were about sixty feet deep, but when they were full, you could reach the top of the mush. Anyway, this fellow was a bit of a lech and as he watched the mags circulating, he was overtaken by furtive urges and tried to fish out a top-shelfer.

But being a stumpy bloke he couldn't quite reach. So he made sure no one was near, moved the safety mesh away and got a chair to lean further over. However, in his frustrated frenzy he must have lost his balance and toppled into the vat, because around an hour later safety officers found just the chair and the open mesh.

There was no chance of him surviving, so the managers decided not to shut down the process, and the mill continued happily churning out cornflake packets.

Another widespread myth, that one. Two nice variations have come to our attention, both, strangely, set in the north-west of England. The first one gives the location as a brewery. The story goes that when the bloke falls in the boiling vat, the factory boss decides it won't affect the flavour of the bitter, and the process continues. (Obviously made up by someone from t'other side of t'Pennines.) The second, and our favourite, has a bloke working in an animal processing plant on the Fylde coast, who is rendered useless

129

by the larding procedure. Again, the line manager decides no one will notice a bit of human in there, and allows the process to continue. The effect on sales isn't recorded.

the carpet *creeper*

Some friends of our family bought a new carpet in the January sales and took full advantage of the offer of a free fitting.

The following week, two scruffy herberts purporting to be carpet fitters arrived in a filthy van to perform the task. Surprisingly, the pair did a fair job of laying the floor covering, and when they'd finished they stood back to have a fag and admire their own handiwork. One of them noticed a small lump right in the middle of the carpet and pointed it out to his partner, who quickly reached for the hammer and with some carefully aimed blows flattened out the bump. Shortly afterwards, the mother of the household came in to thank them, but with a troubled demeanour. 'You've done a lovely job on the carpet . . . but I don't suppose you've seen our hamster hiding anywhere have you?'

The best known variation of this story involves the ubiquitous cowboy workmen and a budgie under the wallpaper, an idea used a few years back in a radio ad performed by Michael Bentine. Another adland urban myth is the Harp commercial, where a new boyfriend throws a ball for the dog in a high-rise flat. The ball takes an unlucky bounce and flies out of the window with the dog diving after it.

plumbing new *depths*

An electrician was on site putting the finishing touches to a brand new detached house on a prestigious new estate. He was connecting the electricity upstairs to start with, working his way down, while the other craftsmen were labouring downstairs.

All morning his gurgling stomach had been playing up after last night's suicidally hot phal curry, so he nipped downstairs at lunchtime to find the toilet and let it all hang out.

All the other geezers were out to lunch – literally – and so the sparkie made his way to the lavvy, took the *Daily Mirror* out of his back pocket and settled down for a lengthy clearance.

Twenty minutes later, he'd finished riding the porcelain Honda, bib and braces around his ankles, and set about doing the paperwork.

Then he stood up to flush the chain – but there wasn't a chain, or a cistern, or a waste pipe for that matter. In fact, the toilet hadn't even been plumbed in yet . . .

incoming *tax*

Some of us are born to genius, others only aspire to being filthy rich. The bloke in this story combined both.

A young postie in Shipley, Bradford, found the job didn't live up to his expectations, and while on his rounds hatched a money-making scheme to set him up for a life of luxurious leisure.

His plan was dead simple. On his patch was a big Inland Revenue office, to which people from all over the country sent off as little money as they could get away with. The plotting postie lived in a quiet village and picked a particularly parochial building society to open up a new account.

Although his friends were impressed by the postie's new-found wealth, they couldn't work out where he'd got the moolah from, and he wouldn't let on. But his Bunsen-burner from the Royal Mail was meagre, and he didn't have any sidelines where he could earn a few extra bob. After a few months, their questions were answered when a warrant went out for his arrest.

Apparently, he'd been intercepting the mail to the tax office on his round and paying it into his building society account . . . opened under the name 'I. Revenue'.

Variations on this popular theme include the postie making deposits under the name 'Inlandia Revenue', or only being caught when he arrives in the works car park driving a brand new bright red Porsche. Another notorious example relates to a temporary employee of the Independent Producers Association (IPA) whose goose was almost cooked when the company toilet over-flowed after thousands of empty envelopes were stuffed down the bowl. The crafty culprit slipped clean away, along with the contents of his building society account in the name of 'Mr Ipa'.

super *fly guy*

In the seventies, our uncle, a mere stripling in the field of employment, landed a job as an assistant in an anglers' shop in Norwich. He was keen and thorough, and the boss loved him for it. So it wasn't long before the lad found himself holding the fort for his employer while the boss went off drinking, philandering or, very occasionally, fishing.

Needless to say, it wasn't long before the boss started to take the . . . well, take advantage, and explained that he'd be off Saturday and Monday due to a long weekend's engagement with a young lady he was instructing in the noble art of fly fishing. So saying, he entrusted his young assistant with the responsibility of locking up the shop at the weekend.

Saturday arrived quickly, and after a brisk day's trade, the lad flipped the sign round to 'closed', cashed up, swept up and turned off all the switches.

Come Monday morning, the keen youth was up with the lark and back at work to open up for trading. He opened the shutters, checked the till and unlocked the door.

The first customer wanted some maggots, so he popped round the back to get them from the cold store.

But when he opened the heavy door, he was immediately made aware of the dangers of turning off the fridge by mistake – a huge cloud of bluebottles flew straight at him, swarming directly into his gaping mouth and choking him.

a miner *tiff*

A mate's dad used to be a pitman in one of the Welsh collieries along with his mates from the same village.

One evening they'd finished a hard day's back-breaking toil, mining a narrow seam deep, deep down in the bowels of the earth. And after crawling half a mile or so back on their bellies, they hitched a lift back to the surface standing on the top of the lift cage, as miners do when there are a lot of others also wanting to fill their lungs with fresh air.

But as the creaking elevator neared daylight, the motor stuttered and the cage, loaded with miners, lurched horribly and violently sideways.

One of the pitmen on top was caught off balance by the movement. He lost his footing and fell off the lift, down towards a mile and a half of pitch-black mine shaft and certain death.

But a quick-witted faceworker in the cage below swiftly lunged over the side, risking his own life to grab down and catch the tumbling miner by the hair – the only part he was able to reach in time. He held on painfully until the others were able to scramble to both workers' aid.

Once safely on the surface, the two men – saved and saviour – locked in a hearty and tearful embrace, and everyone cheered.

Understandably, the event cemented their friendship. They were always talking about each other, visiting and going out drinking. In fact they became inseparable.

But exactly one month after the near-fatal accident, the miner who'd fallen noticed that where his mate had grabbed his hair to save him, the locks were now tumbling out.

Within a day, as if it was in delayed shock, his entire lustrous head of hair was lost. He became as bald as a coot and the hair never grew back.

From that day forward he never again spoke to the man who'd saved his life.

playing *away*

A middle-aged travelling salesman from Salford found himself spending the night in Finsbury Park, north London.

Being frugal with his brass, he sought out a suitably downmarket hotel opposite the park to kip down, though understandably charged his company for a night in a more salubrious venue.

Despite the ropey nature of the hotel, the salesman still wanted the best for his money and tried it on by asking for something 'a bit special, please' when he checked in. The flouncy receptionist winked and said, 'Would you like an extra pillow, sir?'

'Let me see how I get on with what I've got first,' replied the bloke.

135

Then he went upstairs, pushing his way along the corridor occupied by a number of women chatting with what appeared, by the age differences, to be their fathers. He found his room to be a dim, austere single with a clapped-out telly.

Still, he was knackered and it was late, so he flopped down in front of the blinking goggle box.

An hour later, he was ready for bed. Ignoring the dubious round hole carved in the middle of the mattress halfway up, he put his head down. But the pillow was like a sack of marbles, and extremely uncomfortable. He tossed and turned, then eventually rang reception.

'I'll have an extra pillow now, please,' he told the receptionist.

Five minutes later, there was a knock at the door. When he opened it, a voluptuous young lady walked in, smiled and began slowly undressing.

Flustered, the stammering bloke asked her what she thought she was doing.

'You rang for me, didn't you?' she replied coyly.

Apparently, as she explained it, the code in many London hotels for engaging female company for the night is to ask for 'an extra pillow'.

'Damn,' said the salesman, 'shame I didn't ask for two pillows like I normally have.'

Hotels, of course, are better known for what's stolen from them rather than what's provided. It's very common for TVs to go walkies, and mini-bars are there for the taking. (And we thought it was just cutlery and towels.)

Odder, though, were the findings in a survey

a few years ago of what's *left* in British hotels. Apparently, it disclosed that the most commonly abandoned item is, overwhelmingly, the 'girlie magazine'. Next came spectacles and odd socks, and one hotel even reported an unclaimed false leg. Presumably a miraculous recovery had taken place.

highly *unrealistic*

This is how Soviet 'social realism' in art was born.

Just after the Bolshevik revolution, a powerful sultan in one of the old Russian republics asked a local artist to paint his portrait for posterity. When the excited painter went to visit the sultan, he discovered that he might have a few problems making the picture flattering – the war-scarred VIP subject had one eye, one leg and a hunched back.

The artist decided to gloss over the sultan's shortcomings and satisfy his vanity, so he painted him in a glamorous and stirring scene looking the perfect specimen of manhood, surrounded by beautiful women.

When the sultan saw the fictitious representation, he was furious. How dare the painter make fun of him like that, pretending he had no physical failings – he'd be a laughing stock if he stood next to it when it went on display. So he had the artist killed and sent for another.

The second fellow had heard of the sultan's anger and the subsequent fate of his predecessor, and opted for the warts-and-all approach, making a virtue of the sultan's physical flaws. He depicted the sultan sitting in a chair with his eye-patch and lone leg there for all to see, and leaning slightly forward to accommodate his hump.

When the sultan saw this, he was even more furious. How would that look alongside his ancestors' glorious portraits around the palace? And what would future generations make of such a miserable figure? He was so upset he had that artist killed too.

The next painter the sultan approached was a sly old dog with more suss than a Cockney two-card trickster. 'I know exactly what you want,' he told his ruler.

Three weeks later, he presented his work to the sultan, and it was a model compromise of fact, fiction and vanity. He painted the sultan in heroic pose: on horseback, so his absent leg was not in view; facing forward, in order that his hunch would be invisible; and firing a rifle, with the rangefinder obscuring his missing eye.

trouble *brewing*

A work colleague used to be a foreman down on the Channel Tunnel. He had to interview labourers from all over the place for various jobs on the site.

They had plenty of hod carriers, brickies and plumbers, but were a bit short of qualified fork-lift drivers.

The interviews were being held in a damp shed somewhere under the Channel and the first candidate was a very experienced Irish worker.

The foreman always started off with a fun question. 'Can you make tea?' he began.

'Of course.'

'And can you drive a fork-lift?'

'Jeez,' replied the interviewee, 'how big's the tea pot?'

Other Chunnel stories suggest that despite

138

vehement official denials of the thinness of the rock above the tunnel and likelihood of cracking and a flood disaster, all suppliers of cable and electrical installations used in the project were asked to make sure their goods were waterproof (!).

Then there's the fact that although there was a high mortality rate on the Chunnel project, the real toll may be much higher – many of the workers were casual labourers, and no one really kept tabs on how many there were at the beginning and the end.

Oh, and when you ride on the train, don't be surprised if there's a bump halfway across – the French did their tunnelling five feet lower than the British moles, so the tracks didn't meet at the same level. That's why it took so long to complete, but it's all been hushed up.

broom *with a view*

A friend of a friend's dad is quite high up in the civil service, not quite a mandarin but certainly more important than a satsuma. Anyways, he recently had to sit in on an interview panel for internal candidates applying for promotion.

The room was as you'd expect – a well-varnished, oak-panelled affair with a single chair placed in front of a long table, behind which sat the six severe interviewers. Most of the prospective candidates were understandably intimidated and meekly entered the room in alphabetical order.

One candidate in particular was especially nervous. He

stammered his name, then blushed voluminously and was visibly shaking as the panel set about grilling him.

When the interview was concluded, the bloke stood up, thanked the panel profusely with a frog-in-the-throat voice, and whirled round to leave. After a moment's hesitation he marched decisively to the door and disappeared from the room.

The panel looked at each other and after a few minutes continued the interviews until the end of the session. Then gathering their belongings, they vacated the room, leaving the nervous candidate still cringing in the broom cupboard.

so *re-spectacle*

An old friend's mum works in the local hairdressers. Once a week they have OAP specials when old fellas can come and have their tresses trimmed at reduced rates.

Apparently, one day a regular customer, a respectable elderly gent in his early seventies, settled down in the chair for his usual short back and sides. (In truth, he had such a thin thatch it was barely worth his bus fare, but he enjoyed the company in the queue.)

His usual barber was away in Tenerife, so one of the young trainee girls happily volunteered for the job. She was slightly disconcerted when she caught the old gent squinting at her bending over the sink.

But she shrugged it off, and began merrily snipping away and wittering mindlessly about the weather and TV soaps.

A little later, mid snip, the trainee happened to glance down and noticed some disconcerting movement beneath the protective nylon cape she'd put round the old chap. At first she tried to carry on regardless, ignoring his fixed expression.

But again the rhythmic motion caught her eye.

Fetching the old gent a hefty clout, she bawled, 'Cut that out, you dirty old sod!'

'B-but I'm only cleaning these,' the stunned old gent replied, lifting the cape to reveal his polished spectacles.

the cavity *cowboys*

A friend of a friend, a grease monkey, worked for a few weeks as a cut-price cavity wall insulation filling specialist. On their very first day, he and his incompetent mate were called out by an elderly lady in a draughty Victorian terraced house.

The pair clattered up in their hand-painted knackered old van. Then having reassured the poor dear and packed her off shopping, they set about reading the DIY book they'd bought at the market on the way to see what they should do.

The wall that needed filling was found and, grappling with a huge masonry drill, one of the team clumsily bored through until he reached the cavity. Then his partner attached the large foam canister to the injector and began to impregnate the gap.

After fifteen minutes he was still pumping away. The foam in one massive drum having been consumed, the cowboys attached another canister and returned to their task. But within a short time the injecting equipment was once again spitting air.

Something was clearly going awry, but the lads carried on regardless even when the lady of the house returned. A

141

few minutes later, though, their graft was cut short by the exasperated cursing of the old woman. They protested their innocence – what had they done to deserve this?

'Look for yourself,' screamed the woman, pounding them with a brolly and leading them into the adjoining room where she flung open the wardrobe doors.

Sadly, the cowboys had drilled a little too far, and the huge clothes cupboard was crammed to the hinges with solid, yellow, quick-dried foam.

making *a splash*

A new captain was appointed to sort out one of the most unruly ships in the Queen's fleet, and immediately set about improving discipline. But he was a decent fellow and quite fair about how he achieved his aims.

Take the night the crew returned from an evening's debauchery in a tropical Caribbean port – the whole town, in fact, was awash with seamen (it took them days to clean up afterwards). The skipper straddled the top of the gangplank and stopped the sozzled tars with a view to stifling their after-hours drinking.

The first few mariners arrived and their superior subtly reminded them of the alcohol ban, just in case they happened to be trying to bring some on board. Then he gave them the chance to avoid being slapped in the brig, by turning his back and coughing so the sailors might throw away any contraband bottles. Three splashes over the side satisfied him that the chaps had dutifully unburdened themselves, and he waved them on.

Some time later, another couple of salty seadogs teetered shipward, and the captain assumed the position once more, blocking off their hammock access. Clearly these two steamers were the type who loved a tot o' rum, and they were bound to be secreting a bottle or two about their persons to pursue their inebriation. As before he alluded to the fact that his was a 'dry' ship, and suggested there might be something the seamen would like to throw overboard, then he turned his back discreetly.

The wily old tars, plastered as they were, soon provided the skipper with the two splashes he was waiting for. With a satisfied smile, the captain swivelled round to wave the men on board. But as he did so, he happened to glance down at their feet – and saw with some annoyance that each of them had a shoe missing.

supply *and demand*

During the Gulf War, supply ships were the life-line of the fleet. Not just for the obvious reasons – ammo, food, etc. – but also for the officer's libidos, as wives were sometimes allowed to travel on the non-combatant vessels.

It was the practice on one ship for the wives and female members of the crew to take advantage of the warm weather around the Tropic of Cancer by lying out on the deck during quiet moments. One day the male crew of a gunship moored nearby decided to spy on the scantily-clad women as they sunbathed. This was possible by disconnecting the hi-tech sights of the big guns from the centralised, computerised weapons system and using them as incredibly efficient peeping-tom bins.

For a few minutes the ogling lads enjoyed an eyeful of officer class totty. But then a furious officer stormed on to the deck and, red-faced with rage, demanded to know what was going on – the soppy sailors had neglected to disconnect the sights from the guns and all the ship's big guns were trained on to the supply vessel where their senior officers and wives were catching the rays.

punch *lines*

A feeble geography teacher in Stroud was frequently the victim of the subtle wit of one of the most mischievous kids in the school, and driven to distraction in the process. Other teachers were equally exasperated and dished out punishment daily for the errant lad to deliver – 500 lines was the common censure – but the chronic backlog of lines was often their undoing.

The cocky lad seemed immune to such measures and never seemed to do them. Whenever the geography master was pushed to the brink, he would scream at the boy, 'Right! 300 lines: "I must not gesticulate, prevaricate or provide distraction in geography".' At which point the insolent youth would whip out a diary and reply: 'I'm so booked up with lines, sir, the earliest I can fit you in is next April – is that OK?'

shelf-help *scheme*

The local library was moving to the other side of town and, as ever in these times, due to central government prioritising funds to line the pockets of their friends in the City, money was tight for the thriving public service.

But then the chief librarian had a rare brainwave to cut down on transportation costs and encourage increased use by the community. The library encouraged every one of their borrowers to take out ten books each for an extended period – six weeks.

The books were duly returned after the library had moved to its new site, thereby saving a fortune in removal costs.

> While on the subject of libraries, one of the authors (the whispering one) used to work in such an establishment in Hornsey, North London. Among the motley collection of clients there was a woman who used to claim the Russians were coming and that therefore the photocopier wouldn't work (in reality the repairer wasn't coming, which was why the photocopier didn't work), and a man – allegedly a former top-ranking university don – who would rant around the bookshelves, work his way into the reading room, open up the *Daily Mail* and via quick-release trousers that facilitated an easy dump, drop waste on to the centre pages. Always the *Daily Mail* . . . What taste.

badly *stitched up*

A chirpy cockney fisherman who ran a fleet of small boats out of Walton-on-the-Naze made his stash and retired far away in Frinton. As a memento of his life-long occupation and to celebrate the source of his prosperity – jellied eels – he had a fetching wallet fashioned solely from eelskin.

Sadly, the first time he used the new billfold, all his credit cards were wiped clean and he became a pauper overnight. It's a little known fact that eels can drastically affect plastic money – so make a note never to buy an eelskin wallet even if it's going cheap.

going *overboard*

One day at the Mirror Group offices in Holborn, London, Robert Maxwell, who lived in the luxurious penthouse flat at the top, was coming down in the lift. At the next floor he was joined by a scruffy young lad in a suit, who happened to be smoking.

Maxwell was furious that one of his employees should be flouting the company's no-smoking policy – it was a pet hate of his – and he made his feelings known, gruffly telling the office boy to extinguish the weed. The lad sneered and paid no attention, taking another deep draw on his fag and blowing the smoke towards the intimidating entrepreneur.

Maxwell was absolutely livid at this menial's disobedience, and again angrily insisted that he put out the cigarette immediately. The cheeky young man spat 'No!' back at him and carried on puffing.

At this, Maxwell furiously demanded to know how much the young man earned a week. 'Two hundred quid. Why?' scowled the young scamp, as the lift doors opened to the lobby.

'Because,' boomed the magnate, fishing £400 from his pocket and handing it to the bewildered lad, 'I'm giving you two weeks' notice. You're fired! Get out of this building now!'

'Don't worry, mate!' chuckled the rascal, fleeing through the doors with his wad. 'I work for Telecom, anyway!'

last *for Best*

When my uncle re-upholstered George Best's discotheque he heard a curious tale.

George, or Georgie as he was then known, had hit the heights with Manchester United in the late sixties but by the mid-seventies was sadly on the slippery slope down from his former greatness.

A cub reporter keen to cash in on George's fall from grace somehow managed to fix up an interview with the football genius at a swanky London hotel.

The day of the scoop interview arrived, and the reporter turned up on the dot, knocking gently on the hotel room door. It was opened by the great man himself, wearing only a bath towel, beard unkempt and looking well below par.

The reporter entered the room littered with empty champagne bottles. The bed was rumpled, and girlish laughter echoed from the bathroom.

George had been spotted the night before out on the town with yet another newly-crowned Miss World, and judging from the sash and flowers strewn on the deck, one thing had clearly led to another and George hadn't had a wink all night.

The reporter surveyed the scene before him. Then flipping open his note book, he licked his pencil and asked the bemused Best, 'Well, George, where did it all go wrong?'

quite *Frankly*

A friend of a friend knows a bloke who was once in a Las Vegas nightclub with a young woman to see the marvellous

Frank Sinatra in concert. He'd contrived to have a table close to the stairs where 'old blue eyes' walked up to the stage.

Just before Frank was due to go on, the bloke managed to blag his way backstage and talk to the great singer. He explained that his name was Bill, and he'd met Sinatra in the very same club ten years ago when they'd had a drink after the show.

Since that time, the bloke said, he'd married a young lady, but right now they were going through a very rough patch, and he'd taken the liberty of saying he knew Mr Sinatra really well.

'Frank,' said Bill, 'I'm real sorry to put upon you like this, but if you could just say "Hi" or something as you walk to the stage, it would really impress her, and raise her opinion of me, maybe even save our marriage.'

Being an affable sort of guy, Frankie agreed to do so, and as he walked to the stage with the spotlight on him, he leaned over the table where Bill was canoodling with his lady companion and said, 'Hi Bill, long time no see, how are things?'

Bill turned around scowling and snarled loudly, 'Piss off Frank, can't you see I'm busy?'

the bottle *of Britain*

A friend of a friend who's a pilot in the RAF discovered an interesting secret that's been hushed up for over forty years.

During the dark days of the Second World War, when Hitler's Third Reich cast its fascist shadow across mainland Europe, Britain stood fast against the jackboot of Nazi

oppression until eventually the tide of the war started to turn.

Bomber Command's strategy was to pound the Hun into submission and thousands of tons of high explosive were rained down on to the industrial heartland of the Nazi war machine. Day and night, week in week out, the Lancasters and Wellingtons flew sortie after sortie unloading their lethal cargo. Apparently there were so many bombing raids into Germany that the factories couldn't keep up and they ran out of bombs. It would have been a national disaster had the news got out, but luckily the backroom boffins came up with a cunning scheme to maintain the pressure on the Boche until the factories caught up. The RAF switched to dropping empty beer bottles because they whistled just like real bombs on the way down.

Also at this time the government removed the iron rail-ings from working-class areas all over Britain to help with the war effort. Most people thought that due to raw material shortages the cast iron was to be melted down and used to build tanks, ships and planes etc., so they were happy to give up their railings for Britain.

But apparently the whole exercise was dreamt up by the War Office to boost public morale. The railings weren't even melted down, they were collected up, then dumped in the North Sea at night.

Furthermore, the ultimate weapon developed and used during the conflict by the Americans, The Bomb, has been responsible for real shortages of its own. Apparently all X-ray machines have to be made from metal reclaimed from pre-Second World War sunken ships because after the first nuclear explosion and all the subsequent atomic testing in the sixties all terrestrial metals in the world are contaminated by radioactivity.

myth*ellaneous*

Occupations

* Colour-blind people make better bomber pilots, because they're not deceived by camouflage

* Undercover police often pose as artists. You can 'easel-y' spot them by how dodgy the pictures are

* Nuclear bomber pilots have to wear an eye-patch so that in the event of an atomic flash, one eye can still see

* The Bank of England now employs origami experts to check new notes can't be folded in a way that puts the Queen into obscene poses

* In the First World War, soldiers desperate to be invalided out and sent home performed handstands in the trenches, with their feet poking over the top, hoping they would be shot

* Dead sailors fished out of the briny by coastguards are often found to have their trouser zipper undone. It's called 'FOA' – Flies Open on Arrival – in the trade

* Prostitutes join the US Navy as female sailors, enrol on aircraft carriers and make a fortune, sending their earnings back home in conspicuous packages – that's how they get found out

* Russian prostitutes accept share certificates as payment for services rendered

wish *you were here?*

Trouble abroad

The British hate to see other people enjoying themselves, so it's not surprising there are so many urban myths about dream holidays that go horribly wrong. Whether you're a broad abroad or just incontinent on the continent, it's all aboard for a first-class cruise into troubled waters, where most of the travellers come home with only tears for souvenirs. These over-the-top overseas odysseys may kick sand in the face of common sense but underlying that is a pernicious xenophobia, a basic distrust of foreigners and all their parts . . .

the ring of *confidence*

A couple I know went on holiday one year to a hotel in the Mediterranean. They were having a great time until, halfway through their stay, their room was broken into. Mysteriously, nothing had been stolen, though their drawers had been rifled through.

Slightly unnerved they nevertheless enjoyed the rest of their holiday. When they got home, thoroughly relaxed, one of the first things they did was to put their films in for developing – mementoes of the happy vacation.

But the shots they got back provided something of an unpleasant shock. In amongst the pictures of the couple on the beach and in the hotel bar were some revealing snaps showing a rear aspect of the would-be burglars. They were naked, except for the holiday couple's toothbrushes, shoved head-first up their hairy bottoms.

> And remember, the break-in happened *halfway*
> through the holiday . . .

odd *customs*

A mate of mine's dad is an airline pilot. He worked the New York–London run for BA for years and remembers one incident which still makes him chuckle.

He had flown a Jumbo into Heathrow, and when the passengers had disembarked, one of the stewardesses found a little carved box under one of the seats. When she opened it, she found a suspicious-looking powder inside.

Customs staff arrived immediately and one opened the

box, licking his little finger before dipping it into the powder and putting it into his mouth to taste it.

'Well, it's not a narcotic,' he said, efficiently. Just then, an elderly lady came along the aisle and asked the stewardess if she'd happened to come across a small casket containing her husband's ashes.

don't *fetch!*

A bloke I know about knew someone who had a farm in Namibia before independence. It can be tough scratching a living from the African soil, so this farmer decided to diversify, and stocked his irrigation dam with fish.

For a while everything went swimmingly. The farmer enjoyed a diet of fried fish, baked fish, coddled fish – it was fish with everything, and what he couldn't eat he sold at the market for a pretty penny.

The fish multiplied at such a rate they made rabbits look celibate, and soon there were more fish than you could shake a stick at – far too many to catch, and when they started to clog up the sluices and irrigation system, the farmer knew something had to be done.

He happened to mention the problem to a soldier who was billeted nearby to guard the white-owned farms from attack. The squaddy thought he could help. 'Dynamite's the only answer,' he concluded. 'I'll be round at the weekend and we'll blow the bloody things out of the water.'

That weekend, standing at the edge of the dam, the soldier handed a lighted stick of dynamite to the farmer, generously suggesting that as it was his farm, he should have the honour of the first throw. The farmer arched back and hurled the explosive far out into the dam.

But out of sheer habit his faithful labrador leapt straight into the water and retrieved the fizzing explosive, swimming back to the shore.

The blokes ran like billy-o with the hapless hound closing fast, until the dynamite blew, demolishing a nearby chicken shed along with Fido.

Fish feature in another story that appeared in the *Guardian* (down the line from Reuters) in November 1992, and which has all the traits of an apocryphal-tale-turned-news-story. If this isn't an urban myth, it should be: 'An amateur angler choked to death on a live fish, Thai newspapers reported yesterday. Nakorn Hawthong was holding a fish he had caught in his teeth because he did not have a basket, but the fish became lodged in his throat.'

out of the fishing boat, *into the fire*

The boss of my friend's firm was a lover of the good things in life, and one of the best, according to him, was the South of France, particularly the Carmargue. He spent a lot of time there and absolutely adored fishing. One baking hot summer day, he determined to hire a rowing boat and go fishing out in a lake. He found an idyllic, deserted stretch of water, but there were no hire facilities. Luckily, among the rushes he found an old boat that still floated OK and slipped out into the middle of the lake for a fish and a kip holding his rod.

Unhappily, as often happens in the region during hot summers, a hot forest fire blew up a few miles away. The local authorities were alerted and sent for the crop-spray planes to douse the fire with water.

The planes apparently work by flying low over water and scooping the stuff into their holds, then dumping it over the fire.

Our man was still in the land of nod when a plane approached his tiny boat, gathering him up along with several hundred gallons of H_2O, and dropped him, miraculously unharmed, on to the scorching scrub below.

the naked *ski-girl*

A friend was on a skiing holiday in the French Alps. She was having a brilliant time, the weather was fantastic and the snow just peachy. She was a pretty experienced skier and one day decided to go off exploring the slopes by herself. The snow was lovely and compacted with a nice little blow on top.

She was just traversing down an especially fine piste when she was caught short – too much *après ski* the night before. There was no chance of getting back to the lodge in time, and as no one else was around she decided to do it there and then.

Carefully, she unzipped her one-piece designer ski suit and peeled it off down to the knees.

But in the middle of going, she started to move. She'd inadvertently done the 'snow plough' with her skis and was soon hurtling out of control half-naked down the slope.

She ended up in a heap at the bottom of the mountain and was taken to hospital suffering from over-exposure.

In hospital she was relating this story to the man in the bed next to her, in traction with two broken legs, who creased up laughing. When she finished, she asked him how he'd sustained his injuries.

Apparently, he'd been thundering down the slopes when a naked girl on skis had hurtled past, distracting him, and he'd crashed into a tree.

roller*balls*

A friend of a bloke I play snooker with went to Amsterdam for a couple of days, intending to have a wild old time, and take full advantage of the local hospitality.

One stoned afternoon he went to a theatre where there were a number of beautiful naked women on stage, performing tricks on roller skates. The audience were loving it.

For one sequence they needed a member from the audience, and this bloke, ogling at the front, was dragged up by them. They took him to the top of a steep ramp, stripped him starkers and put roller skates on him.

Then a number of the women positioned themselves at the bottom of the ramp and bent over invitingly. He was getting really worked up as he was pushed down the slope towards them.

He shot off down the ramp, and the women jumped out of his way at the last moment, pulled back some curtains and left him to hurtle through open doors into the sunny street outside.

> More variations exist around this old chestnut than there are tulips in Holland. One particular favourite features saucy sailors on leave in Portsmouth. Same plot, though.

welcome *to Dallas*

An Englishman on his first trip to Dallas, Texas, found himself the focus of attention of a liberated, rich and beautiful young woman – they love the accent apparently. She was all over him like a rash, and he was just over the moon. Slightly overwhelmed by her forward nature, he nevertheless invited her back to his hotel room and was thrilled when she accepted.

As soon as they were in the room, she whipped her kit off and dived between the sheets. He quickly followed suit, even removing his socks. When it came to the point of no return, he, being a New Man, instinctively fumbled in his jeans pocket for a latex life-saver.

'Uh-oh,' said the Dallas lady. 'Bare-back riders only with me, cowboy!' So they got stuck in as nature intended.

The man awoke the next day to find that his lover had

slipped away. Smiling and humming to himself, he opened the curtains and ordered breakfast.

It was only when he went into the bathroom to draw himself a bath that he noticed, scrawled on the mirror in gaudy red lipstick, 'Welcome to the AIDS Club sucker! Have a nice day!'

> Of course, before Aids, the same story welcomed the victim to the 'Herpes' club. And before that . . . whatever was the sexual phobia of the day.

the kidney *burglar*

A friend of a friend was on holiday in New York for the first time and, buzzing at the prospect of enjoying the thrills and spills of the world's most exciting city, the Big Apple, checked into his hotel then went out on the razzle. He soon found himself in one of the less salubrious areas, Queens, in a typical New York bar, set up for a night of margaritas and who knows what.

After a few stiff ones, he got talking to an attractive Hispanic woman. She was so vivacious and friendly that he began to think he might break his NYC duck on the first night – and with a real New Yoik chica! When she invited him back to her place he leapt at the chance, though he was so drunk he could hardly stand.

From there on he couldn't remember anything else until the next day. He woke up in a strange bed alone and was struck by a sharp pain in his midriff. Looking down he was taken aback to see a newly sewn wound on his side and rushed out to a hospital, where they immediately gave him an X-ray. He was numbed when they told him that one of his kidneys had been surgically stolen.

> There is medical evidence to support this story in the number of cases of people from developing countries who have recently been willing to sell parts of their body to medical practitioners in the West – in particular the celebrated case of a Harley Street surgeon who had a racket going buying kidneys from impoverished Turks. We've even heard of people selling their eyes in India, and liver donors in Albania. Margaret Thatcher has apparently left her brain to science.

the Empire State *escape*

Apparently, a man once fell from the top of the Empire State building and survived, because he had the good fortune to land on a passing truck full of mattresses.

'hit the deck, *lady*'

Some friends of my parents were on holiday in America, doing a fly-drive package, and decided to spend a few days in New York. They'd been out on the town, done a show on Broadway and had an Italian meal on the Lower East Side. They'd been a bit nervous at first about being in the Big Apple, after seeing all those violent shoot-'em-up cop shows on TV, but now they were feeling quite at home and the service was fantastic.

They drove back to the hotel, pulled up in the basement car park and were waiting for the lift up to reception. It

161

was pretty dark and spooky, the lights were flickering and water dripping, just like the 'Deep Throat' scenes in *All the President's Men*.

Just then a huge black man with a Rottweiler loomed out of the shadows. The lift came and the couple scuttled in. But the huge figure sped up and got inside the lift with his grizzly hound just before the doors closed. Immediately, the black man shouted 'Hit the deck, lady' and the petrified couple threw themselves down on the floor, thrusting all their money upon him, before the lift doors opened and they scarpered out.

Obviously, the incident tainted their stay, and the next day they went to reception to check out. To their surprise, the receptionist explained that a man had already settled their hotel bill, and handed them an envelope.

Inside was all the money they'd thrown at the 'mugger', and a note saying: 'I'm real sorry about scaring you yesterday, and I hope this has made it up to you. By the way, "Lady" is the name of my dog . . .'

> In some versions we've heard, the misunderstood black man is said to be none other than film star comedian Eddie Murphy, some other Afro-American notable like Mike Tyson (honestly, who'd be frightened of him?) or, most implausibly, Lionel Richie! Sometimes he's said to shout the alternative line, 'Get down, bitch.'

the buggering *Bronx Batman*

A friend of a friend called Robin was enjoying a well-earned holiday in New York. He was having a great time in the twenty-four-hour city, and he'd seen all the sights: the Empire State building, Times Square, Broadway, and of course the Statue of Liberty. But after a few days he was feeling a bit lonesome, so he decided to go out clubbing in Greenwich Village and try his luck.

He managed to blag his way into a new hot and hip nightspot but wasn't doing too well. In fact, he hadn't had a nibble all night, until a fabulously attractive older woman caught his eye. She came over to him and they started talking.

He couldn't believe his luck; here he was talking to a beautiful, intelligent, witty native New York, who found Englishmen irresistible. After a few more drinks they kissed – and what a kiss. Then she suggested going back to her place to get better acquainted. He didn't need asking twice.

They caught a yellow cab and took off. She was so randy she couldn't leave him alone. He was gagging for it.

When they got to her penthouse, she practically ravaged him the moment they were through the door, then whispered a suggestion to try something kinky. He nodded furiously. She peeled off her clothes, undressed him completely, and led him to the bedroom where she tied him spread-eagled and face down on the bed.

Then at the crucial moment, a male accomplice burst out of the wardrobe, dressed as Batman, and took him forcibly from behind.

the Mexican *tobacco pouch*

Back in the swinging sixties a friend of a friend in the printing trade knew a sales executive who worked for a large North American paper company.

The salesman had just returned home after travelling around Central America flogging his wares for three months. His wife seemed very pleased to see him back in one piece and after a happy reunion she fixed him a drink and told him to relax while she unpacked his case.

He'd just settled back down in the settee when his loved one appeared at the door holding a heavy duty contraceptive sheath (they were reusable in those days), and demanded to know what it was. Spluttering into his drink, the bloke's mental processes worked like lightning.

'It's a souvenir,' he blustered. 'In fact, it's a Mexican tobacco pouch.' Happy with the explanation the wife toddled off to finish her chores.

The bloke thought nothing more of the incident until a few months later when he was travelling down through South America. It was approaching Thanksgiving and he was feeling a little homesick, so he sent a message down the wire saying he was taking time off for a surprise visit home.

The worried boss telexed back, 'MEXICAN TOBACCO POUCH ON SALE AT CHURCH BAZAAR. STOP. SUGGEST YOU KEEP ON TRAVELLING. STOP.'

This yarn is a real salesman-in-the-pub's 'only in America' shaggy dog story, an old, old classic that seems to have fallen into disuse. We are pledged to putting it back up there where it belongs. The poor old Yanks do seem to come in for some unflattering mythological criticism.

A nice family from Walsall arrived in Los Angeles for the holiday of a lifetime, with the delights of Disneyland at the top of their agenda.

The two young children – a sensible eight-year-old girl and a dozy boy of three – were understandably excited about the prospect of meeting Mickey, Donald and Tron face-to-face, not to mention the numerous death-defying rides in the pleasure park.

The day after they landed Stateside, the family made their first pilgrimage to the Walt Disney theme park.

After they'd been stung for the entry fee, the parents decided they'd done their bit and more or less left their kids to it, taking an easy stroll to just about keep up with them. After an hour of going on everything in sight, Mum and Dad thought it best to grab the kids and get them something to drink.

Their daughter was easily located, but the toddler appeared to have vanished into thin air.

The troubled parents immediately notified a security officer, who took their situation very seriously and swiftly led them to a central control unit crammed with banks of video security camera screens. The sobbing mother began blurting out, 'He's got blond hair . . .'

Gravely, the man in charge interrupted. 'We want you to forget what your son looked like, apart from his face. Just his features, that's all.'

Apparently, after a seemingly interminable ten minutes, the mother shouted that she thought she'd seen her little boy.

They zoomed the camera in to the face of a little child

with black hair, holding the hand of a Mickey Mouse character, who was leading him towards the theme park's exit. As they watched, a group of security guards wrestled the Mickey Mouse figure to the ground and rescued the little boy. A little later, the family were reunited and the dye swiftly removed from the confused little lamb's hair.

Officials later admitted a gang of kidnappers for the slave trade in Colombia's cocaine industry were operating in the park.

However, the family were sworn to secrecy, paid off handsomely and given lifetime free entry to any Disney park in the world – an offer they've still to take up.

Given the concern of many people these days over a perceived increase in violence against children, it's rather odd that this 'white slave trade' myth should be so widespread at the moment. (Then again, myths have always displayed a nasty gallows humour.)

It's a tried and tested formula, with the Disney setting and characters, the dying of the hair, and the 'hushing up' – a common get-out employed by someone who's not too sure of the story themselves – now finding its voice in France with the arrival of EuroDisney. There's something people find irresistible about familiar and trustworthy figures being publicly debased in this way – that's why Parliament was invented.

measure *for measure*

A friend from Australia knows of a property developer in Sydney who bought one of two adjacent vacant plots in the expensive downtown business sector. The developer, who had a reputation as a sharp operator, hired a top architect and erected a huge state-of-the-art glass skyscraper.

Everything was going to plan, with tenants flooding in, when a thick manilla envelope thudded on to the developer's doormat. It was a solicitor's letter from the owner of the adjacent plot, claiming that the new building encroached on his land by precisely one inch. An emergency surveyor was called, and after careful manipulation of the theodolite, his report showed the claim to be true.

The developer then tried to cut a deal to buy off the one-inch strip of land, but the asking price was astronomical – practically the same as he'd paid for the original site. So he wracked his brains for a cheaper way out, and finally hit on a drastic solution. Much to the amusement of the entire construction industry, he hired a team of men to grind the trespassing inch off his building.

The other plot owner was miffed to miss out on the windfall of the developer's error, but decided to erect his own edifice. So a few months later he built a glass tower of equal height and luxury butting right up against the first building.

No sooner was the office block finished than the owner of the first building sent out his own legal threat demanding massive compensation for this blatant encroachment on his land.

Apparently, the cunning fellow had ground not just one but two inches off his building.

167

the taste *of Greece*

The cousin of a friend was on a back-packing holiday around the Mediterranean and was having a smashing time travelling around the Greek islands – Asbestos, Domestos, Bilios, Chillisos, etc. (any more cheap cracks? – no, get on with the story) – until he fell asleep on the beach and woke to find his money and credit cards had been swiped.

The nearest place to get replacement cards and money sent out was a hydrofoil ride away; luckily he'd already booked the trip. So he suffered the whole journey with the lip-smacking smell of moussaka and stuffed vine leaves but no money to buy anything.

When he arrived at the bigger island, he found the bank was closed for lunch, so he tried to take his mind off food, and walked along the seafront.

Inevitably he came to a bar, and there at one of the

tables was a queasy-looking Aussie bloke with a huge pile of spaghetti on a plate in front of him.

The back-packer stopped and looked. The pallid Aussie didn't look like he fancied it, and still hadn't touched the inviting pasta five minutes later.

So the starving traveller plucked up courage and approached him.

'Sorry to ask, mate, but I can't help noticing you haven't touched your spaghetti. I'm starving – I've not had a thing all day. D'you mind if I tuck into it?'

'Be my guest,' belched the Aussie. 'I've already eaten it once.'

midnight *run*

Two friends from work went on holiday to the lovely Turkish holiday resort of Ephesus. The flight had arrived late, so on the first night they had their hotel meal and headed up to their separate adjoining bedrooms for an early night.

In the morning, one of them woke with the lark, looked out of the window at a cloudless sky, and filled with visions of the sea, sand and sights, dressed and knocked for his mate next door.

But when the door opened, it was a complete stranger who stood in his friend's room. The fellow spoke no English, but between them, they ascertained that the other Englishman was not in his room and that the new occupant had moved in that morning. The odd thing was, the room had also been redecorated too since last night.

The concerned man ran down to reception to find out if they knew what had happened – it wasn't like his friend to abscond without warning. At first the hotel receptionist suggested that he must be mistaken, saying no one had booked in with him, which didn't wash at all. Then, looking increasingly nervous, she explained that his companion had checked out first thing in the morning and gone to the airport.

Even more unconvinced, the bloke contacted the airline, who had no record of his friend travelling back, and then rang home to see if they'd heard anything. When all drew blanks, the suspicious bloke called in the police.

As it turned out, he did the right thing: the duty manager of the hotel broke down under questioning and admitted that the English guest had apparently contracted food poisoning from his evening meal, and had been so violently sick in his room that he had died.

They disposed of his body to cover up the incident, and repainted the room to cover their tracks, finally moving a new guest in to try to convince the dead man's friend that he was going mad.

Not every surprise in foreign climes will cost you your life, though.

underground *service*

A friend was in Moscow recently, and travelling on the marvellous and rather grand Russian metro system. What a pleasure it was, he was thinking, to have clean and efficient trains, a regular service and no worries about violence or muggings.

Then suddenly the carriage was invaded by a rough-looking leather-clad gang who guarded all exits to prevent the commuters leaving the carriage.

A man and a woman lay down on the carriage floor and made love in the full view of embarrassed passengers.

Those who turned their heads away had their faces pushed back to watch. A few minutes later the spectacle was over and the gang passed along the carriage demanding money for the show – five roubles each.

One elderly Muscovite protested that she couldn't afford five roubles, so the ruffians only charged pensioners three roubles each.

double *your money*

An epidemic of rumour across west Africa concerned a mysterious stranger. The traveller would appear on the outskirts of a village, and collar one man.

He'd claim he was a marabou, or sorceror, and tell the villager that if he put his money into a magic wooden box, the cash would be doubled.

If he was stupid or superstitious – or both – the villager might put his wedge into the box. The stranger would disappear behind a big baobab tree, warning the man not to look or evil would befall him. And when he came out again, the box would contain exactly double the amount the man put in.

As a special concession, he'd say, if the villager put his family's money in the box, the gods would double that too. The money would be doubled, and the delighted family would be amazed at their luck.

Then the sorceror would suggest – even though he'd

been far too generous already – that the whole village could put their savings in the box, in order to double it.

After the usual deliberations, the villagers and chiefs would put all their life savings in the box. The stranger would disappear behind the baobab with the usual warnings not to follow him, and then not reappear for some time.

The villagers would eventually risk a peek behind the tree, and see the 'sorceror' scampering away hell-for-leather into the bush with all their cash.

wang *end of the stick*

A high-flying executive friend who works for a huge Japanese multinational was enjoying his first visit to the heart of the beast in Tokyo.

One day, he was taken on a tour of the shopping centres, to be shown how Japanese electronics stores' displays compare to those in their UK counterparts.

It was December, but mindful that most Japanese are Shinto and not Christian, the foreign guest was surprised to see that the windows were full of glitzy Christmas themes and tender nativity scenes.

His Japanese guide explained that the shops there use any old festive occasion in order to increase sales, adding that in a few months the stores would be full of Chinese New Year ephemera.

Somehow, though, in one department store, the window dressers hadn't quite got the story right. In an exotic display, the tourist was treated to the sight of Santa Claus in all his glory – nailed to a cross.

dolomite *triumph*

Last winter a couple of mates decided to get away from it all and splash out on an adventure holiday hiking in the beautiful Dolomite mountains of Northern Italy. They were both sickeningly rugged outdoor types bursting with health who thought nothing of running for a bus or climbing a steep flight of stairs after a heavy meal.

The lads were experienced mountaineers and prudently made sure they packed all the right gear – sturdy boots, crampons, cleats, distress flares and, most important of all, a good supply of lumberjack shirts. They weren't ones for taking unnecessary risks.

The first few days were fantastic. They set out on long exhilarating hikes through the craggy topography, scaled mountains and soaked up the breathtaking views.

One day towards the middle of their stay they were well off the beaten path trekking towards a small remote village they'd spotted on the map the night before. The terrain became rockier and rockier as the gradient increased.

Then, as they rounded a bluff it became clear that the isolated village they'd seen on the map was perched on top of a volcanic plug; a wall of solid rock.

Taking no risks, the climbers roped up and began inching slowly up the cliff face in text-book mountaineering style.

The lads were exhausted but flushed with achievement as they neared the summit, and paused to catch their breath. It was at that moment that a young woman from the village flounced past them on her way down, pushing a baby in a pram.

taken *for a ride*

A friend of a very vague acquaintance drives a black cab and often hangs around outside Waterloo Station, hoping a rich American tourist will flag him down and ask to be taken to Edinburgh Castle.

One day his enthusiasm got the better of him when he spotted a couple of confused German holidaymakers who were staring at a rail map and waving their arms about.

'*Sprechen Sie Deutsch*?' the bespectacled husband pleaded as the cabbie forced the ample couple into the rear seat and stowed away their luggage.

'Yer, course mate – I was in the war, weren't I? Where you goin' – hotel, is it? I tell you what, a bit of sightseeing first, eh?' Then the cabbie pulled out in front of an ambulance and was away.

The tourists hammered on the glass and remonstrated as the cabbie wheeled them round Big Ben, then the Palace. So he took them to Harrods, but they still didn't seem satisfied and kept jabbing their fingers at the map, red in the face and yammering things he didn't understand.

Outside Madame Tussauds the taxi driver had had just about enough ungrateful behaviour and pulled back the glass.

'Look mate, what's your problem? Top-drawer tour this, all the sights an' that.'

As it happened, one of the couples' fellow countryfolk happened to be passing and caught their heated drift as it floated out of the cab window. Offering himself as an interpreter, he listened intently to their grievance with a knowing scowl.

'You cheating English *Dummkopf*,' yelled the passerby.
'They only vanted to know where platform 15 vas!'

turned out *nasty again*

A drinking companion from sunny Croydon was on his
honeymoon in Turkey. The weather had been fantastic but
that was about the only thing that had. The compulsory
Turkish massage had been bad enough and in Britain would
have guaranteed the leering masseur a ten-year stretch for
grievous bodily harm, sexual assault and attempted rape
(that was what he did to the bloke – you should have seen
what he tried on the wife). Then he had the cheek to
demand money for the aforementioned offences, claiming
it was healthy.

Next the bloke's stomach started playing up, which after
two weeks of recycled meat-style kebabs wasn't really any
surprise. The state of the facilities wasn't really any surprise
either. Imagine toilets à la Turque (a glorified hole in the
ground), the heat, the flies and worse, much worse,
the embarrassment. These aren't conveniences, they're
*in*conveniences.

One day the Croydonians were well away from the hotel,
being badgered in a 'genuine' bazaar, when the bloke knew
he had to 'go' and fast. The stall owner heard his stomach
complaining and led him quickly to the back of the shop.

It was the worst convenience so far, just a couple of
footprints and a hole in the ground, but the bloke was far
too desperate to care and dropped his trousers and everything else just after.

Relieved, he made use of his pocket full of hotel napkins
and, buckling his belt, pulled the chain. That was his big

mistake. The entire contents of the local sewage system came swilling up around his feet and over his shoes before he could budge. He waded out of the cubicle with the flies hot on his heels.

Smiling weakly at his new bride, he slopped back pitifully to the hotel, his turn-ups full of turnout.

bombay *cow*

Some friends of mine heard tell of a poor Russian fisherman who had nearly been ruined by a most peculiar accident.

Apparently the fisherman was plying his trade on a huge Russian lake, the Aral Sea (he was one of the few Russian fishermen during the Cold War not secretly trying to make whales extinct on the orders of the KGB to destroy Western morale).

This lake is bigger than most small European countries and is like an inland ocean, with tides, storms and pol-

lution, and of course a huge variety of aquatic life to exploit.

One beautiful calm day out in the middle of the lake, the waves gently lapping against the side of the boat, the fisherman was contentedly hauling in his writhing nets when a cow suddenly appeared in the sky from nowhere, smashing right through the middle of his boat and sinking it instantly.

The fisherman was distraught. His livelihood was ruined at one fell swoop of a Friesian. Who would believe such a thing? Certainly not the insurance company, that was for sure, he reasoned to himself as he clung on to a floating spar waiting to be picked up.

Back on dry land his suspicions were confirmed. The insurance company laughed out loud at his implausible excuse. It was the daftest story they'd ever heard. They sent the ex-boat owner away from their office with a flea in his ear and a squelch in his shoes. The poor man turned to drink for solace, his life in tatters.

This remarkable story became the talk of the Urals, and came to international attention. It was then that the embarrassed American embassy privately intervened in the man's life, surprisingly admitting full responsibility for the incident. They bought the delighted trawlerman a brand new state-of-the-art boat with all the trimmings.

Apparently what had happened was this: a huge USAF transport plane had been flying a relief mission in the area and one of the heifers on board had gone berserk, kicking a lieutenant and dribbling on an officer's trousers. In their apoplectic fury the flyboys decided the crazed beast had to go. So they opened the cargo hold and heaved the mad cow out into the wide blue yonder at 3000 feet.

mythellaneous

Travel

* Greek holiday apartment blocks look like they're only half built, because it means the owner doesn't have to pay tax

* It's bad luck to cross the equator twice in one day

* Bikinis are illegal in Turkey

* Postcards of the Queen make good bartering currency anywhere in the world

* Americans think Britain is an island just off New York

* Take a pint of your own blood in a flask for emergencies

* You can sell your blood in Dubai

* In India, they nod when they mean 'no' and shake their heads to say 'yes'

* It is illegal not to wear a shirt in Monaco

* You've got more chance of being arrested in Spain than anywhere else in the world

* In Arab countries: it is rude not to burp in appreciation after a meal; if you like something, they give it to you; the biggest insult is to show someone the soles of your feet

* Koreans sleep standing up for at least two or three years of their lives

* Fijian pearl divers have their ear-drums burst at an early age so they can go down deeper

surgical *spirit*
***

Medicine balls

This catalogue of complaints is a hypochondriac's nightmare and a private clinic's dream. We're all fascinated to hear about other people's medical misfortunes – the more gruesome and peculiar the better. When the malady is closer to home, we're sure doctor knows best. But there's always a fear that if we put our life in their hands, they might just drop it . . .

gone to *seed*

A grubby young lad we knew vaguely at school was apparently sitting at the table eating his tea one evening, when his mother noticed that, as usual, his nose needed attention. 'Go and wipe your nose – and use your hanky,' she boomed. 'But it's not running, Mummy,' he replied.

So his mother called him over, and took her own hanky out ready for action. But when he sat on her lap, she could see, to her horror, that it was actually a small green leaf that was protruding from his nostril. She gave it a little tug, and teased out the end of what was clearly a tomato plant. He had sneezed while eating a tomato some months back, and one of the seeds must have got lodged.

The boy was rushed to hospital where doctors immediately examined him and operated. 'It's a good job we caught it in time,' said one to the mother afterwards. 'A few more weeks and the plant would have penetrated his brain.'

In common with many of the stories in this section, the tomato implant myth is one of those the tabloids fondly turn to during the so-called 'silly season', year after year. It's got just enough horror, just enough weirdness, and just enough credibility as a medical phenomenon to do the business. Look out for these little stories in the papers; they're normally about five lines long, with no names, a vague geographical location (often in the Third World) and no byline. Bored sub-editors who need to fill space love 'em.

four eyes *only*

An optometrist friend knows a nice story that did the rounds a few years back about two brothers who go to the optician. The older boy has been checked and fitted and has come in to collect his specs; the younger sibling is in for his fitting, and is really upset at having to wear goggles. When his senior comes back into the waiting room, the little lad is heartened because the glasses look really good.

But when he sits down in the chair and the 'fun' optometrist puts a cornflake packet, with an eye hole cut out, over the boy's head to test the eyes' relative strength, he bursts into tears. The optician stops immediately and asks the sobbing boy what's the matter. 'I want some like my brother's!' blubs the boy.

the hair *nest*

A girl in the town my mum was born in grew hair into a beehive, as was the fashion in the fifties. But this girl wasn't renowned for her fastidious personal hygiene, and as the hairstyle began to get dirty and saggy, her schoolmates began to notice little movements in her hair and a funny clicking sound.

At first the kids thought it was lice, which were quite common at the time, but when it came to school medical time, the nurse discovered that a colony of cockroaches had taken up residence in her once trendy locks. Later, the story got around that the infestation was actually beetles, and that they'd been boring into the girl's ear, gnawing away at her brain . . .

Bizarre as that perennial apocryphal hair story may be, we've got something to equal it. A friend is always obsessive about removing clippings of hair after having his hair cut. Because, as he says, if you let the little ends stay on your skin, they take root, and you end up with a full growth on your back, shoulders and inside your ears. Elton John, Terry Wogan take note . . .

the back *eye*

My uncle's mate has a glass eye of piercing blue hue. He used to relish an entertaining party trick, but stopped performing it for reasons which will become all too clear in a moment. He would take the eye out of its socket and slip it into his mouth, shocking people by parting his lips so that the eye stared out at them disconcertingly.

However, one time in the pub he was doing just that, but started laughing so much that he choked on the glass eye and finally swallowed it. When he consulted a doctor, the medic told him there was nothing to be done: 'Nature will have to take its course.' Several days later, the same doctor was treated to the sight of the blue eye lodged in the prankster's painful sphincter, staring out blandly.

sticky *situation*

A friend of my workmate's auntie had to pop into hospital for a check-up of a gynaecological nature and was quite nervous at the prospect. She was sitting in the waiting room feeling extremely jittery and in desperate need of the toilet, her nerves having affected her waterworks. So she wandered off in search of a convenience, which was happily nearby. Relieved, she reached out for the paper only to find that, due to NHS cuts, the roll was finished. But opening her handbag, she rooted around, dredged out a tissue and in desperation used that.

When she got back, her name was called. Shortly she was surrounded by inquisitive medical students and a crusty old consultant who told her to open wide. Incredibly embarrassed, she nevertheless did as bid. There were gasps and guffaws from the students, so the consultant came down hard on one giggling youth.

'What's the matter, never seen one before?'

'Yes,' he spluttered, 'but never with a stamp on it.'

wagging *it*

A friend of my uncle's owns a really mad mongrel dog, a proper Heinz 57; not dangerous, but nutty as a fruit cake. It's got one of those wagging tails that only mongrels have: always whipping from side to side, knocking ornaments off shelves and that kind of thing.

Anyway, one day the dog was leaping about in the kitchen while the bloke was scraping its dinner out of a tin. Unfortunately the crazed beast caught the table-cloth and dragged their best china on to the hard tile floor, smashing the lot.

The bloke was so furious that he lashed out at the mutt with his foot, but missed, slipped and fell down hard. He landed heavily, right on his coccyx – the small triangular bone at the base of his spine. It was awfully sore for days and still throbbing a week later, so he went to the doctor.

The quack was stunned. The blow had somehow trig-

gered a primitive growth hormone and the bone was grow-
ing into what it had been in primeval times – a prehensile
tail. In a queer throwback, the bloke ended up with a
stumpy tail-like growth. He could wag it and everything . . .

pea *soup*

A district nurse in Sleaford, Lincolnshire, had on her regular round an elderly woman who was always griping about
the quality of social service she was given.

Talk about looking a gift horse in the mouth! Nothing
was good enough for her, from the type of dressing on the
sores on her hips, to the places the council arranged pleasant
day trips to.

But the churlish woman reserved her most withering
criticism for the meat 'n' two veg supplied by the local
'meals on wheels' service.

One particular afternoon, the fresh-faced nurse arrived
in particularly fine spirits, determined not to let the old
biddy grind her down as usual. But as soon as she was in
the door, the old grouch was whingeing on about the food
she'd been served earlier.

'Look at that!' she thundered, pointing a wrinkly finger
at a garden pea on the side of her plate. 'What d'you think
that is?'

'Well,' said the nurse, trying to remain cheery, 'it's a pea, isn't it?'

'Is it?! *Is it??!!*' said the woman, even louder. 'A bullet more like. Just you feel it!'

The nurse walked over and gently squeezed the minuscule green vegetable. The old woman was right; it seemed rock hard.

'There! Just you try and chew it, see what I've to put up with,' ordered the old mare. So the district nurse picked up the pea again, warily placing it inside her mouth and bringing her jaws to bear on it.

With a 'ping' the pea shot out of her mouth and bounced around the room and off the china horse collection.

'See!' barked the old woman. 'And it's been through me too!'

from *beer to eternity*

A bloke from Staffordshire was visiting his sickly uncle in hospital. The older relative had just had a serious operation, but he was only too pleased to polish off his nephew's get well gift, a couple of cans of beer – though it was strictly against doctor's orders.

Sadly, the next day the uncle was found dead in bed.

'That's ironic,' remarked the nephew on hearing the news. 'Because the beer I took him was Long Life.'

as *directed*

Our family knew the husband of a health visitor in London's East End, who had some odd stories.

One involved an old man on his wife's 'beat', a crotchety

fellow suspicious, like so many of his generation, of all medical professionals and their prescriptions. Because of this fear, he often withheld information about his health problems, almost until it was too late.

On one such occasion, the health visitor saw him wince as she was about to leave, and prised out of him the fact that his bottom hurt. A quick inspection ascertained that he had a severe case of haemorrhoids. A few days later, the health visitor visited the elderly gent with some suppositories to ease his 'Chalfonts'. He huffed and puffed, but grudgingly accepted them and agreed to follow the instructions on the pack.

The next week, when she came to visit the old bloke, he was even more surly than usual. She asked him if his piles had improved. 'With those things you gave me! Course they bloody haven't,' he snapped.

She asked him if he'd followed the directions. He just scoffed. 'It said "Place in your back passage", but I don't have one, so I put them in the hall. I might as well've shoved them up me bum, for all the good they've done!'

> N.B. For those who choose not to flavour their speech with an East End patois: according to the lexicon of cockney rhyming slang, 'Chalfonts' is short for 'Chalfont St Giles', which of course rhymes beautifully with piles.

getting *the point*

A friend of the family had been suffering for some time with a nagging back pain. After trying all the traditional methods of treatment to no avail, he decided to try alternative medicine and visited the local acupuncturist. The practitioner was a highly regarded but faintly mysterious old man who'd been practising in the area for years.

On the day of the appointment, the suffering patient was sitting in the waiting room looking around, feeling a little nervous. But his nerves were calmed by the Cantonese certificates of qualification, which were very impressive.

The first treatment didn't hurt at all and fixed his back pain a treat, so much so that the patient began to go regularly for relief.

As it happened, the next time he paid a visit there was an Oriental gentleman in the waiting room. The bloke got talking to him, and asked him how he thought this chap compared with the real thing – Chinese acupuncturists back home.

The inscrutable old man replied, 'He's very good indeed. The only thing that concerns me is why he has a licence to sell fish in Hong Kong harbour on his wall.'

body *and soul*

An acquaintance I once met at a party recently heard a strange tale from the Emerald Isle. Apparently, if you have a limb amputated in an Irish hospital, it is carefully buried in the hospital grounds. Then when you eventually shuffle off this mortal coil, no matter how many years later, you are buried alongside it.

> It's not known what happens should you be unfortunate enough to have more than one limb amputated and buried in different parts of Ireland. Perhaps there's a limb processing centre for the

recently deceased, assembling all the parts in the correct order before burial. An early reference to this practice of reassembly before burial may be hinted at in the phrase 'bury my heart at wounded knee'.

tijuana *flu*

A young, free and single Surrey man was on the holiday of a lifetime in Mexico, thoroughly enjoying himself in the pursuit of melanin enhancement and local talent. His only problem was a streaming nose that developed after a few days, but he was prone to hay fever and the arid Gulf breeze had clearly done its worst, so he wasn't unduly concerned and kept the Kleenex handy.

One night, he found himself in the company of a dusky maiden at the bar of a romantic nightclub, and was trying his best to impress. His opening lines worked a treat, and she was bowled over by the fantastic stories of success and adventure he related (all about himself, of course). His banter was quality, and things were progressing nicely.

Then he proposed a toast to their 'fortuitous meeting' and took a hefty swig of his cocktail. The brown-eyed Mexican damsel's mouth dropped wide open in horror. She stared wide-eyed at him, blanched chalk white and careered off, hand over mouth, into the night.

The bloke was mortified. What could have shocked her so? He felt his face – nothing amiss – and his tie was straight. He resolved to leave and try his luck elsewhere. Looking in the Martini mirror behind the bar to check his appearance, he lifted his glass to down the dregs. As he did so, he spotted with rising panic two browny-yellow and slimy slug-like parasites slip out of each nostril and dip their feelers into his margarita, and then slither their way up again when he jerked back his head in horror.

just *earsay*

An old school friend of my auntie met her in the street in Cleckheaton the other day and sadly related the tale that their old geography teacher had recently passed away.

The old chap had been a marvellous advertisement for his profession in his earlier years but apparently of late he'd become more and more dotty and had been obliged to take early retirement.

It wasn't until his sudden death and the subsequent post mortem that the reason for his deteriorating behaviour became clear. It seemed that a number of years before, on a geography field trip, an insect had drilled its way into one ear, through his brain and out through the other lughole.

The parasite had been discovered and destroyed, but no one realised it had laid its eggs in the middle of its journey. The hatched-out grubs had been eating his cerebrum ever since. By the end, sadly, he couldn't tell his ox-bow from his elbow.

finger-*licking good*

A friend of the bloke who lagged our hot-water tank used to work deep in the bowels of Bart's Hospital in Clerkenwell, torching boil dressings and other medical waste in the incinerator. His job involved visiting the various wards

and operating theatres, emptying bins and taking away rubbish sacks.

It was on one of his forays that he came across a consultant from the urology department instructing a white-coated bunch of fresh-faced students. The well-scrubbed gaggle of undergraduates was crowded tightly round the donnish consultant eager to soak up learning. He had a small petri dish in front of him containing a sample of urine, and was discussing testing for sugars in the body and their medical implications.

'In fact,' he enthused, 'one of the simplest tests we can do for excess sugar in the urine is the taste test.' The students shrank back cringing, but he insisted the human tongue was capable of detecting sugar quite accurately, and to prove it he quickly dipped a finger into the yellow fluid, before popping it into his mouth and nodding vigorously.

Then he made each squirming student in turn dip a digit in the 'sample' and taste it thoroughly, before asking, 'Right then – hands up who saw me switch fingers?'

myth*ellaneous*

Health

✳ Rainforest Indians have a cure for every disease known to man, but pharmaceutical companies sponsor gold prospectors to wipe them out so we never hear about them. If the public heard about these simple remedies, the companies would be put out of business

✳ If you experience a strong sensation of smelling oranges for no reason, it means you're just about to have a brain haemorrhage

✳ They can repair literally anything with key-hole surgery these days

✳ Sit on wet grass, cold stone steps or a hot radiator, and you're bound to get piles

✳ A bloke who was deaf in one ear once lost his digital watch somewhere in his bedroom, and was driven mad by not being able to find it when the beep went off every hour

✳ When laser surgery is in progress in an operating theatre, new nurses often complain about the smell of sizzling bacon

✳ Have all your teeth pulled out and you'll never suffer from arthritis

✳ A hospital in Edinburgh had an electric shock treatment machine fitted and reported fantastic results. When an engineer came to service it after a year, he found it hadn't been connected to the electricity

✱ Breasts grow to fit the size of your bra, but the breast over the heart is always bigger than the other because it gets more blood

✱ Everyone has a relative who's 85, has smoked and drunk all his life, and is as fit as a butcher's dog

✱ Whenever you've got a gynaecological problem, you're booked in with a GP of the opposite sex

x-rated

On-the-job jams

A little carnal knowledge is a dangerous thing. And so is love, according to this *menage à* try-anything-once from our world-renowned Institute of Scatology: this alternative lovers' guide poses more sexual dilemmas than Rod Hull and Emu. The flesh may be weak, but the punters are gagging for it.

kinky *K.O.*

A quiet Nottingham husband and wife, friendly with a workmate of mine, were determined to spice up their humdrum sex life. To this end, the bloke timidly visited a Private Shop in town, and came home with some pretty raunchy bondage gear.

They couldn't wait to try it out and within the hour they had it on. The wife was fastened to the bed in a star shape, while the husband elected, for some reason, to climb on top of a wardrobe, pretending to be a big cat moving in for the kill.

But at the crucial moment, he leapt down, hit his head on the bedframe, and knocked himself out cold for several hours. It fell to his unfortunate wife, still fastened in full tackle to the bed, to alert the neighbours so they could break in and set her free. The cul-de-sac was never as quiet again . . .

lovers' *lock*

In the late seventies, two young people were making love in the back seat of a Mini (yes, it can be done), when due to a sudden muscular contraction and seizure, they were stuck fast. Luckily the woman was able to reach round her partner to press the horn and summon help. Soon after, the fire brigade were called, but try (and laugh) as they might, they couldn't liberate the lusty couple.

Eventually, there was no alternative but to cut the top off the car with oxy-acetylene gear and winch the still locked-together lovers out. The woman was in floods of tears, and a fireman tried to console her by explaining that there was nothing embarrassing about their predicament: 'We see things like this every day.'

'I know that,' said the woman, 'but what's my husband going to say when he sees the car . . .'

a sad *reflection*

Someone at work knows a quiet bloke who one day furtively asked someone else in the office if they had any hardcore porn videos he could borrow, as he'd got hold of two machines, and could copy them. He was lent one, and took it home to copy. But he wasn't too *au fait* with the workings of video recorders, and couldn't work out how to copy them direct.

Eventually, he resorted to what he knew: he set up his camcorder on a tripod and pointed it at the screen, recording the film as it played on his telly. When he returned the video to the lender, he explained the problems he'd had. So when he got home, the other bloke checked that the video he'd lent was all right. He was more than a little displeased at first to find out that the bloke had given him back the copy, not the original, but his annoyance soon turned to mirth.

The copy was a very poor recording, with a terrible glare from the TV screen, but as he looked closely, in the reflection he could make out the distinct image of his workmate kneeling in front of the box, gratifying himself.

> Often linked – unfairly, we tend to think – with the omnipresent carrot-topped celeb Chris Evans. Strangely enough.

chicken *gobble*

A father was renowned for staying out late and falling asleep in front of the telly in a drunken stupor. It got to such a state that his teenage kids used to stick things on him when he was asleep.

One night, they got the neck from the giblets of a chicken they'd had for dinner, and placed it in their drunken father's fly, dangling down. In the morning, his wife nearly had a heart attack when she saw the cat licking and chewing what she mistook for something of a more intimate nature.

fit for *nothing*

Apparently, when someone suffers an epileptic fit, one of the main problems is that the victim's teeth clamp shut for the duration. That's why it's sadly quite common for epileptics to bite through their tongues.

Anyway, I heard about a couple who were out on Lovers' Lane one night in their car. Their motor was too small for anything but oral relief and they'd got up to a '68-er – 'You give me a blow-job and I'll owe you one' – with the woman seeing to her man first. Tragically, while *in flagrante delicto*, the woman suffered an epileptic fit and her jaws clamped horribly shut. In his pain the bloke tried to loosen her vice-like grip, unavoidably bruising her face rather badly. Eventually the fit passed and they drove painfully to hospital where they had to answer some awkward questions from smirking nurses about the injuries they'd sustained.

tits *first*

When I was a DJ in Newcastle, one of the regular clubbers told me a story about a Geordie lass he'd encountered.

He was dancing in the club and chatting up a real bonnie lass, who was coming on strong. He bought her a drink and they had a good laugh together. Shortly, she whispered that they should go back to her place, which they did.

So they were sitting on the sofa and the lad's hand started to wander up the Geordie girl's thigh. Suddenly she broke off, slapped his face and shouted indignantly:

'Where's yer manners, like? Tits first!'

revenge *is . . .*

The husband of a woman my wife works with told me about a friend of his from home in Norwich who'd gone out to a disco with his mate. They'd all been drinking heavily to build up their courage, before seeking out the local talent in Cinderella's Nitespot. Before long they all tapped off – it was that kind of place – except this one bloke, who just kept on necking the ale all evening.

At the end of the night, he'd managed to strike lucky with a lass, who he took back to his place. They undressed and went to bed, even though he was really slaughtered and having trouble even raising a smile – let alone anything below the belt. After a few minutes foreplay, his head began to spin and, disappointingly, he threw up all over the woman and passed out flat on his back next to her. When he woke up, with a splitting headache, he was alarmed to see there was a small turd lying cleanly on his chest, but the woman who put it there was nowhere to be seen.

the botty *bottle*

A friend who's a porter in a casualty ward was one night alerted to a commotion caused by a throng of nurses, some peeling away, hands over their mouths, to stifle the laughter, surrounding a terrified-looking bloke crouching face-down on a stretcher, and covered by a blanket.

It transpired that he had an old-style milk bottle firmly implanted up to the lip in his back passage. The victim explained that he'd been taking up some curtains in the kitchen when he'd slipped and sat on the bottle, which was upside down on the draining-board.

The force of his tumble had formed a vacuum and to remove the vessel, the surgeon only had two means at his disposal: either smash it, or find the means to get some purchase and pull it out. He decided on the second course, and carefully filled the bottle with plaster, slipping a stick inside before it set rock hard – a bit like making your own ice-lolly, really. Then, straining hard, he tugged it out with a pop.

Two weeks later, the same man was back with a similar problem – only this time, he'd 'fallen' on an old-style Coke bottle.

bangkok *Bill*

An Ashford, Kent, man went on business to Bangkok for a month, and took enthusiastic advantage of the local hospitality. Perhaps too enthusiastically – for after a week, he found his three-piece burning up with some strange infestation. Immediately he visited a clinic specialising in communicable diseases. He was diagnosed as having crab lice and had intensive, expensive treatment for the rest of his stay.

When he returned home, he decided not to come clean with his wife. But as luck would have it, one morning she was opening his mail over breakfast as usual and came across his American Express bill, which she always pored over with extra care.

This time, one particular entry caught her eye, and she called upstairs quizzically, 'Darling, what did you have done at the Bangkok Institute for Sexually Transmitted Diseases?'

> Sex and religion – an intoxicating mix, full of
> innocence, guilt and holy inappropriate
> behaviour . . .

more cake, *vicar?*

A friend was a bit of a handful, in more ways than one – but more of that later. Anyway, he recently started a relationship with a lovely girl. Although they'd been going out for quite a while he had never been introduced to her parents and was very keen to meet the old fossils. He knew the father was a man of the cloth, but fancied getting a shufty at the old dear to see what his girlfriend would turn out like. The girlfriend seemed determined to prevent a get-together, probably with very good reason.

Then one day, out of the blue, she suggested going to her parents' house to sort through some of her old school things. He couldn't wait. However, when they arrived at the house he found, to his disappointment, that his girl-friend had arranged for her folks to be out. They went up to her bedroom and started sorting through the bric-abrac. But one thing led to another and they ripped off their clothes and made mad, passionate love rolling around on the old exercise books, then dozed off.

A little later, he woke up on his own and, still naked, set out to find his girlfriend. When he got downstairs he could hear her in the front room listening to the radio. The door was slightly ajar so he decided to have a bit of fun. He propped up his abnormally large John Thomas between finger and thumb, waved it round the edge of the door, and squawked in a high-pitched Mr Punch voice, 'That's the way to do it! That's the way to do it!' There was no reaction so he did it again. Still silence, so he popped his head round the door.

There, frozen amid the vicarage tea and cakes, was his girlfriend, red as a beetroot, and her astonished parents.

the party *pooper*

A mate went to art college, leaving home for the first time, and early in the first term he went out to a humdinger of a house party in a dodgy bit of Liverpool.

He'd taken his carrier bag of cheap cooking lager, and soon got into the swing of the drunken revelry. Psychedelic music thumped out, students writhed by the light of joss sticks and – even better – there were *girls* there.

Midway into the evening, the room started to spin. It could have been the lager, or the iffy, fish-scented footy-burger he'd had on the way up, but the freshman's bottom was telling him he was in dire need of the toilet.

The queue for the lav in the house stretched all the way upstairs, but there was no way he could wait (or risk the noise he'd make with people standing outside). Then he

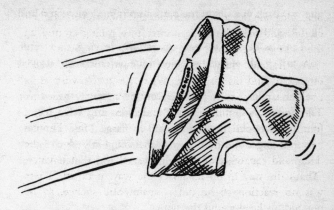

remembered there was a small loo downstairs in the hall and made a mad dash.

Happily, it was quiet below the party, though the toilet was fusty and dark. After a noisy delivery, the lad reached for the paper, but – nightmare of all nightmares – there was no bum-fodder.

Terrified of humiliation, he sat there quaking, stinking and thinking hard. Then a drunken thought occurred to him. He took off his paisley Y-fronts and used those as a sanitary wipe, flinging them into the porcelain bowl and flushing the handle triumphantly.

But to his horror, when the toilet water cleared the soiled shreddies were still there, steaming in the pan. A couple more cistern-busting flushes produced the same result, so he fished out the Ys and tried another method of disposal.

Opening the door a crack and checking there was no one around, he ran through the front door and hurled the sopping, stained knickers out into the street. Minutes later he was back upstairs in the party humming, convinced he'd got away with it.

Later as he and his new mates were leaving, they came across a gaggle of party people on the pavement and strolled over.

The students were gathered around a heavily-soiled pair of sodden paisley underpants and discussing what sort of dirty sod could have done such a thing. Then someone noticed the old school name label diligently sewn in by mum on the hem of the pants, and read the name out aloud . . .

below *the belt*

A friend's cousin was getting married, and his mates organised a drunken, seedy stag do above a pub in Stockwell, south London, for a dozen of his close mates. It was one of those stag nights you only seem to *hear* about, never get invited to. They'd organised some raunchy videos to start with, then at about 8.30 the 'girls' came on. Three local strippers did a live sex act on stage, and towards the end of their performance, they grabbed some of the lads (the ones wearing ties) and gave them the 'towel' treatment. Then they dragged them up on the stage and made them do all sorts of filthy things with their clothes off. After the act had finished, some of the lads approached the girls about providing something a bit more private, and negotiations were carried out. Eventually, the drunken groom-to-be chatted one of them into giving him a blow-job for an extra £5. They adjourned to a side room, and he was given a quick seeing to. But his hand began to stray under the skirt of his partner, and to his horror his fingers encountered two hairy plums. The stripper was a man . . .

mr and *Mrs*

A friend of mine was at a wedding reception that was a real laugh. The stag night was mad enough, but at the reception after the ceremony they did a 'Mr and Mrs'-type question and answer quiz with the bride and groom, asking each in turn intimate questions about the other, who had his or her ears covered while this was going on.

First to go was the groom, a right cocky so-and-so. They asked him various things about his new wife, and then:

'Where's the most unusual place you've had sex?' That really got people going.

'Easy,' said the groom, 'on the kitchen sink.' There were howls of embarrassed laughter. So they brought the bride back, a shy girl who didn't like this at all. Everything went OK until the same question.

'Where's the most embarrassing place you've had sex?'

The bride went as white as her dress and looked over to her husband distraught, whispering, 'I can't, I can't.' He was laughing his head off and said, 'Don't worry, love, I've already said. It's OK.'

Still not sure, the bride turned and answered: 'Up the bottom.'

> That one really has been doing the rounds recently, and we've been told at least five different versions. All those who told it swore they were there, of course, but does Derek Batey know what a huge cult he's made of himself?

mr Blobby *on the job*

A woman set up her husband for one of those impromptu home invasions Noel Edmonds' shows specialise in while she was 'out with her mates' one Saturday evening. On the show, the cameras burst in and start filming, to the surprise of their unsuspecting prey.

The TV crew secretly case the joint before they begin filming to make sure things run smoothly, and this time it was a good job they did. With the wife who'd contacted them standing nearby, the production crew peered through the living room curtains to check what their victim was up to and make sure he didn't suspect anything.

It was quite soon clear the husband wasn't expecting anything, let alone a TV crew to burst in and film him.

For him it was just another Saturday night without the missus. He was sitting on the couch with his trousers and underpants down, holding a can of beer and playing with himself while watching *Baywatch*.

> Chris Evans offered a good deal of dosh to anyone who could produce the footage 'proving' it was him. Easy money! (Only joking!)
>
> And – sorry about this – yet another couple of self-gratification stories. Firstly a quickie about a friend of a friend, who as a pubescent teenager used to lie in his bath watching a woman through the bathroom skylight in a flat opposite. Even though she seemed to be looking at him, the mature lady was quite clearly oblivious to his voyeurism and used to undress virtually every time he had a bath. Naturally, he would excitedly

stimulate himself accordingly. When he grew up, he became a respectable surveyor for the local council and happened one day to be working on the estate where he'd grown up, now deserted. As a sort of pilgrimage, he paid a visit to the flat of the woman of his childhood dreams. He was quite disturbed when he did, for he found out that from the spot where she would stand and disrobe, his old bathtub was completely exposed to her gaze.

rub-*a*-*dub*

A spotty teenage youth from Kent was enjoying a long languid bath and, having soaped and scoured himself, had begun to get quite aroused.

Needless to say, he decided to relieve himself while still soaking. So he leant on his arm until his hand went dead (that way he could pretend someone else was doing it), and finished the job.

But just as he climaxed, his mum knocked forcefully on the door and told him to hurry up. She wanted to use the same bath to save water (there was a shortage), and she was in a rush. Appalled that his mum would see the conspicuous floating evidence of his vice, the young man spent a frenzied two minutes stalling her while he fished out the flotsam. When he'd done so, he rushed out and let her in.

Happily, there was not a peep from his mum. But nine months later, the lad had mixed feelings about his mother giving birth to a new brother for him.

the genital *touch*

There used to be a pub in Newcastle-upon-Tyne just off the notorious Bigg Market cattle-run that had rock'n'roll as its theme, but in a sordid, downmarket way – tacky pictures of Elvis, Eddie Cochran and Tommy Steele, I seem to remember.

But the main attractions in this rowdy drinker were the waitresses, dressed in scanty swimsuits. Every so often the lasses were made to dance, gyrate and cavort on top of the bar to certain songs on a backing tape, with the lusty hordes clapping along with their tongues hanging out.

Apparently, one night, following a particularly exuberant hoofing display, one of the waitresses, who happened to have active genital herpes at the time, rearranged her costume. Then she immediately resumed serving the leering punters, unwittingly passing her affliction on to every cocktail and pint glass she handled.

As a consequence, thirty or so men contracted clusters of genital herpes around their mouths – something, you can imagine, quite difficult to explain away to their partners . . .

> That one's been cruising the bars all over the country. Any regional variations? We'd love to hear them.

her *pedigree chum*

A Surrey businesswoman woke up on her 40th birthday with the usual misgivings and feelings about advancing years. A divorcee, she received just a few cards from her family and went to work feeling very lonely.

At work, no one seemed to have remembered her big day, and no one even asked her out for a celebratory drink at lunchtime or the evening – in fact, they all seemed to leave early.

So she trudged home forlornly, and went through the side gate and round the back into her kitchen as was her habit.

Unknown to her, all her workmates and neighbours had arranged a surprise party for her and were lying in wait in a hushed huddle in the living room.

But when she didn't emerge from the kitchen for twenty minutes, the organiser, her next-door neighbour, decided to check she was all right.

So she sneaked over and eased open the louvre doors to take a peek.

There, lying naked on the floor, was the blue-stocking birthday girl, with dog food smeared all over her body and her pet Labrador enthusiastically licking it off.

the bus *seductress*

Back in the swinging sixties a paint-spattered fine-artist friend from Dunfermline was kept waiting at his bus stop for an inordinate length of time and only found out the reason the next day.

The regular bus driver on his route had recently been joined by a young clippie who he'd immediately taken a shine to. She was a fine looking young lassie and had customised her uniform to conform to the mini skirt fashion of the day. As a result the bus was always full of working men, many travelling way past their usual stops.

The driver, a young chap himself, had taken to wearing

an open-necked shirt and powerful aftershave and insisted on personally showing the young clippie the ropes. She was not immune to his charms and despite his acrid cologne they soon became close friends – very close friends.

But there was an impediment to their young love. Both of them lived at home with their parents and it was hard to get time alone on their own. So they took to making the beast with two backs in the empty double-decker after the last run on a Friday night, when it became their own little passion wagon. It was just the ticket, though probably against company regulations. Their sessions also included some of the shortest rides the bus ever experienced.

One hot summer Friday evening the young driver's passions became particularly heated and as he yanked on the handbrake in the deserted garage, his love wrenched open the door and pounced on him in the cab rather than waiting for their usual back-seat tryst.

Close to the end of the line, though, they experienced a fearsome 'lovers' cramp' and became inextricably coupled.

They were still jammed together the following Monday, when they were discovered by the raucous early-morning shift who immediately phoned the sniggering Fire Brigade to cut them free.

balls *bounced*

A friend has a story about two mates at his rugby club. One day, the two were having a post-match shower as usual when one of them bent over, and the other one was heard to exclaim, 'Cor, the size of your ball-bag, mate.'

The embarrassed bloke was forced to admit his secret –

by a freak of nature, he had been overendowed, by one, in the testicular department.

When he'd recovered his composure, the other fellow suddenly had an idea. At the pub they were going to, there was a barman who would bet on absolutely anything, no matter how impossible – he was a bookies' dream, a real mug punter. The bloke hit upon a scheme to earn them free drinks all night.

They arrived at the boozer and the insatiable Billy Bunter barman was there for the taking. They played it cool for a minute, then the rugger player leaned over the bar and whispered into the barman's ear: 'Betcha, between you and my mate, you've got five bollocks.'

The barman gave him an old-fashioned look. He repeated the bet. The barman began to smile, and the bloke knew he'd got him.

They settled on a wager, and the barman disappeared into the toilet, followed by the three-ball rugby player.

But to his surprise the barman swiftly undid his kecks and dropped them, saying defiantly, 'There's my one, where are your four?'

massage *virgin*

A friend of a bloke I know works in an insurance office, where he sits opposite a portly middle-aged bloke with sweat permanently peppering his top lip.

This shiny-arse was a bit of a hypochondriac and was never slow to complain about his ailments. His regular gripe was a painful ache between his shoulder blades, brought on he reckoned by his high stress duties – paper shuffling.

A workmate sick to the back teeth of the malingerer's

whining suggested he try a massage to relieve the tension and recommended a place nearby. The bloke was hesitant at first but said he'd give it a try. That lunchtime he popped out early in search of relief.

The massage parlour was just off the high street: it looked clean and bright, and the professional neon sign was most encouraging, so he scuttled inside. He was soon flat on his belly with only a towel to preserve his modesty.

The lithely-built oriental masseuse got stuck in straight away, kneading and pummelling in all the right places. To the bloke's astonishment, the pain disappeared almost immediately and he began to relax and thoroughly enjoy the massage. So relaxed was he in fact, that the firm hands working on his body started to have a stimulating effect, and he was soon feeling more than a little aroused.

When the comely masseuse asked him to flip over she couldn't help noticing his conspicuous excitement. So she whispered furtively in his ear, 'Would you like a wank?'

The bloke thought for a second, then nodded furiously.

The masseuse winked and left the room, and the bloke lay back, his head filled with mucky thoughts awaiting her return in who knows what exotic costume.

But a few minutes later, the masseuse popped her head round the door and said, 'Have you finished yet?'

He'd obviously got the wrong end of the stick.

lady *luck*

A bloke of 30, yet to lose his cherry, consulted his best friend over how he could pop his cork for the first time. His mate mulled over the best means: prostitute? – nah, his

pal was too sensitive a soul for that; lend him his own wife?
– she'd never agree, hated the bloke. Then he remembered
a woman he'd been told was free and easy with her affec-
tions: a 'sure thing'. It was decided that a blind date should
be arranged, and this was duly done.

Naturally, the 'quarry' was nervous on his date, but had
to put that behind him when he stopped off on the way
at the chemist, just before it closed, for a packet of rubber
johnnies. Mustering all the bravado available, he trousered
up to the counter and blurted, 'Better give me a 12-pack,
I'm feeling lucky.' The attractive young assistant smiled
coyly, and the bloke rushed out as quickly as he could.

A short time later, the optimistic bloke was sitting in the
chosen restaurant, clutching a bunch of flowers and a folded
newspaper as arranged. A few minutes later, his blind date
turned up. To the pair's mutual embarrassment she was the
young woman who'd served him in the chemist, and it was
quite obvious to her what he was after . . .

hamming *it up*

A well-known practice among gay men in Los Angeles – and some Hollywood actors, it's said – of slipping a hamster or gerbil up their partners' back passages (this apparently provides a highly pleasurable stimulation while the rodent scurries about) took a violent twist once when two loving partners tried it.

One bloke introduced the hamster into his mate's orifice, and awaited the moment when the ecstasy would become too much and he would have to retrieve the burrowing creature.

When this moment arrived, the bloke held up a piece of cheese to lure the hamster back out. But it wouldn't emerge, and the 'host' was in real pain. Panicking a little, his partner, who looked through the love door but couldn't see Hammy, racked his brain for a solution.

All at once he had an idea, and fumbled around for some matches. Then he lit one of them and held it close to the other bloke's bottom, hoping to shed some light on the situation and locate the errant rodent.

But by chance there was a build-up of gastric gases inside the 'host', and these were ignited by the flame. In a flash, the hamster was discharged from between the bloke's buttocks like a bullet from a blunderbuss, hitting the astonished partner full in the face and breaking his nose in two places.

beeb *boob*

The BBC once had a woman newsreader, well-liked by the public but the butt of many back-handed comments from crew and backroom staff over her penchant for picking up young men after OBs (outside broadcasts).

She was the model professional on screen but, especially in her early days, like an unbridled mare on heat as soon as the red lights went out. When a story took her away from home and into hotel land, with all its possibilities, she was bound to pick up some local lad for a good rooting.

On one occasion, the crew decided to set her up. They were shooting in Manchester until late, and the filming went well. That evening, the crew waited until the presenter nipped out on the prowl as expected, and then wired up her hotel room, trailing the microphone leads into an adjoining room, where the recorder was positioned.

Sure enough, cometh the late hour, cometh the young man. The sound engineer in the adjoining room picked up the sound of the door shutting and then two voices. The lovers got down to business almost immediately, and the crew next door were creasing up at what they heard.

Nothing, however, prepared them for the memorably unguarded remarks of this household name while in a state of complete abandon. At a crucial moment in the love throes she was heard to shout, 'Fuck me, fuck me, fuck me till I fart!'

> Quite seriously, we have heard that story associated with three different women newsreaders – some more plausible than others, if you get our drift, but none verifiable ... no matter what BBC people say to the contrary. Another of Auntie's classics suggests that the late PM Harold Wilson once threatened to close down the BBC if he was interviewed 'rudely' again. All caught on camera, of course.

corporal *punishment*

For some years it had been the habit of squaddies stationed at Huntingdon barracks to make a stop-off on their way back to camp after a Saturday night skinful. The regular port of call was a chemist's shop letter box, through which they would prod their percies and urinate several pints of recycled Best.

The chemist was understandably aggrieved, and determined to teach the soldiers a lesson they wouldn't learn on the parade ground.

Checking his watch, the pharmacist stationed himself just inside the doorway as the pubs shut. Sure enough, a bunch of squaddies rolled round the corner and headed for the chemist's as usual.

When the first one chuckled and thrust his todger through the slot, the chemist was ready with his sharp tweezers to inflict an alarming injury. Worse still, the soldier's hasty retreat from the sharp, spring-loaded letter box meant the flap bit off more than even a Thai pleasure girl could chew, and that's a lot, apparently.

the bishop's *wife*

A friend was well acquainted with the daughters of an eminent and popular bishop who sadly passed away a few years before his wife. Now she too has gone to join him beyond the pearly gates.

In his youth the bishop had answered a calling to the Far East and spent many of his formative years in the post of missionary. His wife had accompanied him there and together they spent many happy years in missionary positions throughout the Orient.

During this time the bishop's worthy wife was presented with a striking bronze medallion heavily decorated with mysterious Chinese characters and complete with chain. The cleric's spouse was so taken with the medallion that she wore it always and noted with considerable satisfaction the fascination it never failed to arouse in company. Strangely, the ornament seemed to open all kinds of doors; people seemed to want to get close to her. She put this down to the medal's talismanic effect which evinced a studied awe from Eastern intellectuals.

Despite this obvious and knowledgeable interest she never managed to have the medal's curious inscription adequately deciphered. Scholars she questioned always claimed to be unfamiliar with the nuances of that particular Cantonese dialect.

But now she'd popped her clogs and her daughters held no such love for their departed mother's prize possession. The medallion was up for auction with her other belongings. But it seemed even now to have the power to intrigue, and was definitely the most talked about item in the auction.

Not surprisingly, really: the catalogue entry read 'Three-inch-diameter solid bronze Chinese medallion. Early twentieth century Cantonese inscription reads (transl.) 'City of Shanghai Registered Prostitute No. 179'.

trouser *snake'n'vac*

Obviously every nurse and hospital porter has his or her story of a late night kerfuffle, and a friend working in

Birmingham still winces at the thought of one night when things were quite quiet and suddenly a fellow was brought in on a stretcher with a huge sheet draped over the middle of his body.

Naturally the staff's morbid curiosity, er, I mean, compassion, was aroused and they approached the patient one by one to see what they could glean, er, do to help.

The bloke had nearly bled to death and the reason was clear. They'd brought him in with a sheet over him because he had a short vacuum cleaner attachment still stuck firm on the symbol of his manhood.

Or what was left of it. In a bizarre solo sexual effort, the young man had fastened the domestic appliance to his one-eyed monster and switched it on. Sadly, it was rather a new model and the efficiency of its sucking action was such that his dong was extended as far as the machine's rotor blades, and he was now half the man he used to be.

And that's why all the hoses now have clips that let air in and break the vacuum.

> Before inadequately equipped gentlemen rush out to test such a member-extending tool, they should bear in mind that sometimes the polarity has been known to suddenly reverse on such machines so the contents of the dustbag are blown back up.
>
> Every Casualty department in every town has its share of 'objects of desire' stories and we've certainly detailed a few in our previous books, but this tale of bumfoolery has a rather nice twist. (Unless you're the patient in question!)

behind with *the milk*

An ex-boyfriend of a friend used to be a medical student and was working in the Casualty department of the local hospital when a fellow claiming to be a window cleaner was rushed through in obvious agony.

The poor man was face-down on the stretcher and had a milk bottle firmly wedged up his back passage.

The doctors and nurses had seen this 'rear entry' type of thing many times before and tried to keep straight faces as the window cleaner ran through his tale. Apparently he'd been up his ladder, wringing out his chamois when he'd slipped, flipped over in mid-air and landed legs akimbo on top of the empty gold top.

The sniggering staff were convinced the story was a concoction and that the bloke had been indulging in some perverse act or other.

One buttock-relaxing injection later, the empty milk bottle was removed. To everyone's astonishment it clearly contained two perfectly punched-out circles of fabric, one from the window cleaner's blue denim jeans and the other from his red nylon underpants.

a relative *shock*

Deep in the Texas panhandle a young couple were caught camping out in an area of desert where such things are strictly forbidden. Although it was dusk the eagle-eyed Texas Rangers had spotted a flashlight and headed across country in their patrol vehicle to confront the miscreants.

The young guy heard the engine and ducked out of the canvas begging for leniency. Coming clean, he admitted they'd run away from home but were both just under-age, even though recently his voice had dropped and his balls had broken(!). The grizzled patrolmen were in a quandry about what to do when the youngster popped back in the tent and, after a hurried discussion, came up with a novel solution to the problem.

Apparently the teenage girl in the tent had offered to perform oral sex with the Rangers if they let the couple off. It had been a hard few hours on the road and the grinning cops readily agreed.

The sergeant cockily let the younger patrolman go first, to save time, so he reckoned. A few minutes later it was the sergeant's turn and, to the sound of his zipper bursting open in anticipation, he entered the tent – only to come face to face with his own daughter.

express *your love*

A friend regularly travels by InterCity Silver Service – like standard class but with a paper tablecloth thrown in for an extra thirty quid each way. One day she got chatting with one of the stewards she fancied and he told her about an incident which had occurred only a few days earlier on his mate's 125.

It was the midnight run down from Edinburgh to London and the train was fairly empty. One young couple who'd obviously had a bit to drink were in a semi-empty carriage, snogging furiously. They didn't even look up to have their tickets punched.

The couple's lascivious passion became more and more inflamed and, not content with heavy petting, their carnal desires ran wild and they began making mad, passionate

220

love on the table. Blissfully engrossed in their hedonistic performance, they hammered away over the points, until they parted, exhausted, and slumped back into their seats.

Then the bloke struck a match to light a post-coital cigarette for his love. Oddly, it illuminated a lewd thong of leering faces. They'd watched the whole licentious performance in silence, but now decided to make their presence felt, tut-tutting and pointing to the 'no smoking' signs.

nec-*romancer*

The elderly undertaker in a small Derbyshire town had kept a secret for years. To the public he was a sombre, upright man of dignity who always keffed of formaldehyde; by night he was much more upright than they imagined, and was in the habit of acquiring carnal knowledge of the cadavers in his charge.

To his suppressed delight, one day a distraught family asked him to handle the funeral arrangements of their dearly departed eighteen-year-old daughter. Solemnly taking delivery of her corpse the undertaker drove, skipping red lights, back to his parlour.

As soon as he arrived, he gave his assistant the afternoon off, drew all the curtains, turned the door sign to 'closed' and jumped naked into the lovely young woman's coffin. Then he had his wicked way with her.

Midway through the necrophilic act, the late lass shockingly shot bolt upright, coughing and screeching, and clearly not very dead at all. The undertaker tried to disguise what was going on by quickly applying a screwdriver to the casket, but to no avail.

When the parents discovered what had happened, they revealed that their daughter had been in a coma after a crash and had been pronounced clinically dead – wrongly, as it proved. The shock of the funeral director's intrusion stirred her back to life, and the family were so grateful they declined to press charges against him and the whole thing was hushed up.

Sex

* It's got a bone in it

* Oriental ones go sideways

* Ra-Ra-Rasputin, Russia's greatest love machine, was actually impotent. A doctor who examined him in 1915 found his 'parts' shrivelled

* Some sheep-shaggers turn the animal round in their wellies so as not to miss out on the kissing

* Shag a sheep on a cliff: it backs up

* In the First World War, two-thirds of the men fighting had some form of venereal disease

* Legendary porn actor King Dong fainted through lack of blood when his pendulous member became erect

* The large penis gene is dominant, and as a people we are getting bigger

* Most blokes could tell you where the 'G-spot' is

* If a bloke masturbates too many times in one day, only a whistle of air comes out

* The *Kama Sutra* was first translated by nuns

* Whenever there's a power cut, nine months later there's a population explosion; the biggest baby boom ever occurred nine months after England won the World Cup in 1966

friends *and relations*

Nowt so queer as folk

From the cradle to the grave there are myths for every milestone on the highway of life: even if you survive your young brother throwing you out of the window, the ropey rituals of a rocky marriage, and the best intentions of your mates, you've still got the perils of old age to look forward to – and dread.

atlantic *potion*

As is quite common among British families, my pal's parents in Essex had an elderly aunt and uncle in Canada who had emigrated decades earlier. The *émigrés* retained a nostalgia for home, but at the same time felt they had bettered themselves and tried to help out their kin who stayed behind by regularly sending them examples of the good life they enjoyed in the new world, like food or electrical gadgets.

One year, nothing arrived for a long, long time. The family began to wonder how their Canadian folks were, but correspondence remained unanswered.

Then after several months a package arrived from Canada. It was a Jiffy bag containing a little box with what looked like powdered soup inside. How typically sweet of them! But there was no note with the soup, so the family drank it still unaware of how their aunt and uncle were.

Two days later, an air mail letter arrived from Canada. It was from their aunt, apologising for not keeping in touch, but explaining that she had spent all her time nursing her husband for the last six months before he died.

On his death-bed he had made her promise that he would be buried on English soil. 'But I couldn't send his body back, so I had him cremated. I sent his ashes in a separate parcel, and I know you'll see to it that your uncle is given a suitable send-off,' concluded the letter.

Just after the Second World War, it was common-place for relatives who'd been evacuated or emigrated to Canada or Australia to send food parcels back to rationing-hit Britain. The sort of thing in the last story happened all the time. Nowadays, the ex-pat relatives are renowned for thinking younger members of the family they left behind are stuck in some kind of pre-pubescent time warp, and sending thirty-something cowboy suits and *Cat in the Hat* books for their birthdays. That's Canada for you.

a fart amongst *friends*

A Fulham lass my wife's sister knows is always getting herself into scrapes, usually over new boyfriends. This occasion was no exception. She had just met a really dishy posh bloke, who had invited her to a party with his friends. Determined to impress him, she dolled herself up in a tight, classy little black number.

At the party, though, she was so nervous that a certain amount of biliousness welled up inside her and threatened to make itself heard in the form of a loud trumpet, so that she couldn't relax at all. What made it worse was that every time she tried to give vent to her flatulence in private, her guy sought her out with a smile and sidled up next to her. The queue to the lav stretched down the stairs, so no point in waiting for that either.

Eventually, her boyfriend came over to her and said, to her relief, that they were going now. Holding in the noxious wind for just a little longer while the bloke escorted her to his car and let her in, she was even more relieved when he finally left her side, saying he'd forgotten to get someone's telephone number.

With immense satisfaction, she sat in the passenger seat and let fly the most enormous rasping fart.

A minute later, her man opened the driver's side to get in. 'Sorry, I've been terribly rude – have you met Carol and Peter,' he said, pointing to two embarrassed friends silently holding their noses in the back of the car.

> With tasteful adjustments, that scenario was used in the TV sit-com *Just Good Friends*. But this next one was obviously beyond salvation; Jan Francis' danger money would've been too high . . .

that sinking *feeling*

The same young lady, apparently, was involved in an equally excruciating episode with another posh bloke. On this occasion, she was invited to the young man's swanky Knightsbridge town-house to meet his parents. She'd never been to a really big, upmarket mansion, and she was on her best behaviour.

It was a very formal meal, and everything was just so until she needed to use the toilet. Worried that asking for the 'lav' was crass and common, she tried to recall the posh way to say it. Then she remembered, and asked her boyfriend's mother 'for the cloakroom'.

The mother gave her directions to an upstairs room, but when the young woman opened the door, it was exactly that: a cloakroom with coats, etc., but no toilet, just a small wash-basin.

By now desperate for a leak, the lass hitched up her taffeta dress and jumped up to sit over the sink to relieve herself. Halfway through, however, there was a nasty crack and the sink came away from the wall. The huge crash was heard downstairs and the diners rushed up to check on their guest.

When they opened the door, they found her sprawled over the smashed porcelain with two painfully twisted ankles, and her knickers round her knees, in a suspicious-looking puddle.

> Both these stories epitomise the powerful element of class conflict in apocryphal stories, and the idea that you should 'stick to your own' and not get above your station. Social climbing it seems, always ends in a fall.

the old man *and the teeth*

My uncle's a bit of a fisherman and he knows a bunch of ancient anglers – all of them must be over seventy if they're a day – who like to go off on fishing weekends to get away from their wives (which is a relief for their wives too). One time they decided to try their luck at sea-fishing off Grimsby and set off early, in a convoy of old bangers.

Unfortunately, the briny started to cut up rough into a heavy swell as soon as the crusty old codgers were afloat. The boat was pitching and rolling and they all felt pretty green. One particularly queasy old gimmer lost his breakfast over the side, and with it his false teeth, to his great annoyance and the huge amusement of the others.

Later, when the sea was much calmer, another old bloke hooked a large mackerel. For a joke, he slit open the fish, took out his own false choppers and slipping them inside, called to the bloke who'd chucked up, 'Would you believe it? Look: this here fish swallowed your teeth!'

'Give it here,' said the choppery old fogey, snatching the set of teeth, and slipping them on to his gums. Then he grinned, spat them into his hand and chucked them over the side, saying, 'Naw, they're not mine.'

down *the hatch*

This actually happened to a friend of mine from Camden. He was round at his girlfriend's parents' house for the first time, and they were having a very polite meal together.

Nerves (and a beans-on-toast luncheon) were playing havoc with him and he had an untimely case of bad wind. Excusing himself, he swiftly left the table and rushed to the toilet, but on the way spotted a little open window and simply thrust his bottom through the hole and guffed loudly.

Shortly, he returned to the silent dinner table. The rest of the evening passed without mishap, for which my mate was very grateful.

In the car on the way home, the lad turned to his quiet girlfriend and said, 'Well, I thought it went very well. What d'you reckon, darling?'

'I reckon it was going fine until you farted through the serving hatch . . . darling.'

go *ferret*

A Barnsley lad kept ferrets and enjoyed nothing better than to carry one round in his trousers. Contrary to popular belief, the creatures don't bite or wriggle. The motion usually just makes them lie still, giving a warm glow to your nether regions.

Anyhow, this lad was one day courting a lass, and opted for taking her to the pictures. It was only when he picked her up on the way that he remembered he still had one of the ferrets down his kecks.

He was aware that the lass might be quite shocked by the grubby rodent, so he resolved to keep it in his baggies for the duration. However, towards the end of the film, as they tucked into the last of their snacks, the lass felt someone having a good go at her popcorn.

'Bloody cheek,' she thought, annoyed at her boyfriend, 'he's just polished off a packet himself.'

But the attack on her popcorn continued, and she slapped her hand down to stop him – and screamed alarmingly. Just then the house lights went up, and the lass screamed again.

There was the ferret, stretching out of the lad's flies, still tucking into her sweets.

> Why do people put ferrets down their trousers?
> It's got to be risky, but probably a lot less risky
> than a mongoose in your boxer shorts. (Think
> about it . . .)

phone *home*

A double-glazing salesman in south London was ringing a contact telephone number he'd been given, and the receiver was picked up immediately at the other end. A tiny voice whispered:

'Hallo?'

'Hallo, can I speak to your daddy please?' said the caller.

'No, he's busy,' replied the little voice.

'Your mummy, then. I'll speak to her.'

'You can't. She's busy too.'

'Is there anyone else there?' persisted the caller.

'Yes,' the voice conceded, 'a policeman, but he's busy as well.'

'Anyone else?' The caller was now getting a little exasperated.

'Yes, a social worker.'

'Well, can I speak to the social worker, then?'

'No, she's busy too,' said the soft little voice.

'Look, you've got all those people at your house and they're all busy. What are they *doing*?' asked the caller.

'Looking for me,' came the whispered reply.

naïvety *play*

The friends of a family we know have a precocious eight-year-old who counted as his girlfriend a little girl who attended the same school.

During the Christmas term, the kids were selected for parts in the traditional nativity play. The boy was extremely upset at the casting: his girlfriend landed the part of Mary, but he didn't get to play Joseph opposite her. Nevertheless he took his role seriously and all the rehearsals went smoothly.

Come the big night, all the parents were glowing with pride as they watched the heart-warming performance. Cushion-pregnant Mary and her carpenter husband Joseph duly arrived at the inn with their wooden horse and asked if there was a room for the night.

It was the little boy's big moment, and he didn't disappoint.

'Course you can, Mary,' he shouted, grabbing her by the arm, 'but Joseph can sod off!'

> Apparently, later in the same play, Mary was tending to the little doll, new-born in the manger, when one of the shepherds haltingly asked what she was going to call the infant. Mary dried for a minute, thinking hard. Then her face lit up, and she replied, 'Julia'.

passing *out*

A mate from Preston was taking his GCSEs at the local comprehensive. One particular lad in their class, a bit of a swot, was swaggeringly confident about his grades right up until a few weeks before sitting – after that, the nearer the day of reckoning drew, the clammier his palms became.

When the first day of examinations actually dawned, the lad was quaking in his boots. The reluctant fifth-formers trooped into the dusty hall, checking the notes on their sleeve cuffs hadn't smudged, and set about strewing biros, assorted gonks, Snoopys and sundry lucky mascots about their desks.

The worried lad squirmed in his seat, flushed hot and cold, and began shaking slightly. When the examiner asked them to turn over their papers and begin the poor boy's head was swimming. He glanced at the questions, then panicked.

He put two sharpened pencils up his nose, leant back, then smashed his head forward on to the desk, which drove the pencils up into his brain and killed him instantly.

Needless to say the other shocked candidates suffered an even worse fate – they had to sit the exam all over again at a later date.

a friend *of the family*

A guy at work commutes to the office in west London by express coach. For years he shared the journey every day with two other blokes from the same village in Dorset, and the three of them would sit together and jaw all the way to reduce the boredom.

Then for a few months the guy was working elsewhere and didn't travel up to London.

When he next had to commute to the Big Smoke by

coach, he was quite surprised to see the two old friends sitting apart; one at the front, one at the back.

He only really liked one of them, so nodding to the other, made his way to the back. Naturally, he asked why the mates were avoiding each other.

The bloke sighed, and related his story – he was a broken man. Apparently, some time ago the other commuter, Fred, had split up with his wife, and, feeling sorry for him, the storyteller, Sid, had invited him around for dinner. They'd had a great night, but Sid got a little concerned when his sixteen-year-old daughter appeared subsequently to have a crush on his mate, always asking after him and when he was coming round again. A little later she began mysteriously disappearing in the evenings and avoiding her parents' questions about where she was going.

On his daughter's seventeenth birthday, a few weeks later, Sid arranged a surprise slap-up dinner for her, but was dismayed to hear she'd already arranged a date.

'Who with?' he demanded. After a little sheepish stalling, the young belle admitted it was Fred. The ensuing confrontation ended in tears.

Incensed, Sid rang up his old pal to put things straight.

'Look,' he pleaded, 'you're old enough to be her grandad. Please, leave her alone before you break up my family.'

A few weeks later, ferreting around his daughter's room, Sid came across a love letter – from the dreaded Fred – which read, 'I spoke with your dad last night, and he told me to leave you alone, but I still want to keep our dates as usual, and I'm glad you do too.'

The two friends had a showdown the next day in the scene of so many happy times, the coach. They sat down next to each other.

'Look me old mate,' Sid began, 'this is breaking up the family, it's coming between me and you, and it's not doing anyone any good. It's got to stop.'

'Which one?' said Fred. 'Your daughter or your wife?'

home *and away*

An impressionable young woman working for a London PR firm met the man of her dreams at a press launch. He was so smooth-talking, so sincere and kind, so funny too, that she was swept off her feet and didn't really notice that she was being plied with drinks.

He seemed a well-to-do sort of bloke, with a motor to match his mouth, and the woman allowed herself to be driven home by him in his flash car after he'd filled her mind with all sorts of glamorous stories about his playboy lifestyle. Not wishing to appear unworldly, and feeling more than a little tipsy, the lass found herself not protesting when he said he was taking her back to his place.

Half-dazed by the champagne and this whirlwind suitor, before she knew it the young woman was hanging on his arm as they walked briskly along the dark road to his house. It seemed an unusually quiet street, but she'd guessed he lived in a select neighbourhood. He fumbled for his key – she vaguely remembered thinking it was quite sweet that he was nervous too – and then hissed, 'Don't turn on the lights, it's more romantic in the dark.' The couple's frenzied passion knew no bounds. Their discarded clothes marked a tangled trail to the master bedroom.

The next morning the young woman was woken by the sound of embarrassed voices – there was no trace of her moonlight lover. But gathered at the end of the bed were a red-faced estate agent and a handful of prospective buyers shuffling uncomfortably.

All became horribly clear when the young woman spotted a big sandwich-board sign just outside the window that read 'Executive Show Home – View By Appointment Only'.

a smashing *honeymoon*

The brother of a bloke I work with planned a lovely summer wedding to his childhood sweetheart.

A plumber by trade, he was a bit worried about any pranks that his mates might play – especially after the wicked stag night, where he'd been stripped naked, covered in boot polish and handcuffed on to the night train to Inverness.

But the wedding went off blissfully and after 'Birdy Song'-ing the night away they slipped off to their elegant country-house hotel retreat for the wedding night nuptials.

The car was decked out with the predictable balloons and shaving foam, but the groom was still worried; things were going all too smoothly.

The couple checked in and were led up to the honeymoon suite. The groom was still nervous and insisted on checking the room for hidden microphones – it would be just like his mates to bug the room.

It was the bride that found it – an oversize bolt head, badly concealed under one of the big Indian rugs.

The vindicated groom scuttled down to the car and returned with his tool kit. The couple were finishing screwing the large bolt out of the floor when it suddenly went loose.

Moments later they heard a deafening, shattering crash, as a priceless antique chandelier fell from below them and smashed into smithereens on the lobby's hard marble floor.

five-*year hitch*

Some friends of our vicar, a perfect, lovey-dovey couple, had lavishly celebrated their fifth wedding anniversary.

Then one day the wife caught her hubby whispering furtively into the telephone. He slammed the receiver down as soon as he saw her, but couldn't conceal his embarrassment.

The couple had a blazing stand-up row, with the wife accusing her husband outright of having a covert affair. The flustered geezer blew his top, refuted the accusation vehemently and slammed the door behind him as he stormed off to the pub.

Blubbing into her hanky, the cunning spouse carefully lifted the receiver on their modern telephone and pressed the last number redial button.

A tearful woman's voice answered at the other end. Her worst fears confirmed, the wife blurted out, 'You rotten cow, how could you steal my man away from me? We've been happily married for five years.'

The other woman retorted, 'Never mind that! How d'you think I feel? The swine's just finished with me after seven years!'

take *a chance*

A woman who had been dutifully and hopefully filling out her pools coupon for more years than she cared to remember was amazed one Sunday morning to see in her paper that she was at last amongst the winners with the maximum 24 points. She exploded with joy and straight away told her equally exhilarated four-year-old son and her husband, who gazed heavenward and looked like the cat that got the cream.

On the Monday, the husband went to work as usual, his head buzzing with the prospect of all that loot. But they didn't know how much they were due, and his wife had said she'd ring up the pools company to check as soon as the office opened. At lunchtime, the husband expectantly rang home to hear the result. His son answered, saying Mum had had to nip next door for a minute.

'D'you know how much money she's won, son?' asked Dad.

'Yeh, about £66,000,' chirruped Son.

After that, wild horses couldn't have halted the bloke as he rushed out of the office and drove straight to a car showroom where he'd seen a smart peacock blue Escort XR3i with soft top. Sure enough, the motor was still there, and the bloke negotiated an HP deal and a trade-in for his old banger. Then he rushed and drew out his life savings in lieu of his wife's forthcoming wedge, and that evening he drew up outside their terraced house smoking a big Cuban cigar and honking his horn in the spanking new four-wheeler.

His wife stepped outside and, smiling cautiously, asked where he'd got the money from to buy it.

'Well, it can come out of your pools winnings, can't it?'

'But I rang to check, and they said I'd only won £1.60,' said his wife.

The bloke looked distraught – all his life savings up in

smoke. He stammered, 'But when I rang up earlier Jimmy said you'd won £66,000.'

'Oh my God – he was talking about our Monopoly game.'

privatised *depression*

A social worker mate in Glasgow had to visit a woman who's been put through the mill due to the incompetent Tories' recession. The worst slump since the 1930s had decimated her life. Nothing was going right.

The company she worked for had sacked her and then gone bust, so she'd had no redundancy money after sixteen years' service. Her husband had lost his well-paid job in the building trade and they'd fallen way behind on their mortgage.

The house was about to be repossessed, but it had plummeted in value so they owed the building society more than it was worth. The car and all the furniture on HP had been taken by the bailiffs, and every letter was a final demand.

Finally, the strain of living on the breadline had wrecked their marriage and her husband had left to build a new life for himself down south. It was the last straw; the poor woman had had enough, and decided to end it all. So she opened the oven, stuck her head inside and switched the gas full on.

But she woke the next day with a stinking headache, to find the gas supply had been cut off.

paper*boy*

A husband from Peckham, who'd spent too much time on his work and felt he'd been neglecting his wife, one day resolved to turn over a new leaf and do right by his missus.

So early the next morning he told his surprised wife to have a lie-in – he'd collect the paper and fetch her breakfast in bed.

Feeling good about himself, the bloke heard the paperboy approaching and collected the paper, but as he turned away from the letter box, he felt a cold hand goose his bare backside.

Furiously, he opened the door and rattled off some choice words to make quite sure the over-sexed teenager never reached in and groped his wife again.

Neighbouring curtains twitched, but he didn't care who heard him.

Then he noticed his cold-nosed labrador standing next to him, and realised he'd stupidly mistaken its affectionate greeting for the paperboy's.

pole-*axed*

A friend whose girlfriend caught him *in flagrante* in bed with another woman came home to find his live-in lover had quietly but unsurprisingly flown the nest.

For a few weeks he revelled in his new bachelor status, then invited his new lady to share the flat. After a few weeks of freedom the apartment looked awfully untidy and a pungent pong had taken root in the bedroom.

Apparently, the jilted girlfriend had stuffed an economy packet of party prawns inside the curtain poles. No matter what they tried – the great smell of Brutal, disinfectant everywhere, joss sticks, changing his socks – the nostril-attacking niff remained, worsening by the week.

Over the summer months, the whiff had graduated from a honk to a genuine hum, and very fishy it was too.

In fact the smell got so bad that after changing all the furniture the couple decided to move out. The endemic stench meant they were forced to accept a price for the flat far below market value, but they were happy to be leaving the pong behind.

It just so happened that the former girlfriend got wind they were moving out and was passing as they were packing the van.

With great pleasure, she watched the removal men take down the brass curtain poles and carry them into the van bound for the new apartment.

There are many other vengeful stories of this ilk, often associated with jilted lovers. One tale has the spiteful former paramour sowing watercress in a carpet (most entertainingly in the bathroom carpet, where a fresh crop appeared after every shower). Another story concerns two lads with a rudimentary knowledge of motors but a master's degree in mischief, who put a rotten fish in the ventilation system of their mate's car. After a few days, especially when the engine warmed up, the whiff got pretty bad, and the poor bloke shampooed his carpet, bought Feu Orange and everything (he was convinced it was something his friend's dog had left in there), to no avail. The funniest part was, until his mates broke the news, he was turning the ventilation on full to try and purge the pong, which of course only served to make things that little bit worse.

robin *red-face*

A young Irish couple who'd been courting for some months went out for a romantic evening topped off by a visit to the pictures to see the blockbuster movie *Robin Hood – Prince of Thieves*, the all-action historical romance starring Kevin Costner.

It was a touching film, very tender, and the devoted couple especially loved the smoochy theme song, 'Everything I Do, I Do It For You', crooned by Bryan Adams. Later the same night, as they listened to 'their' song in a local pub, the boyfriend went down on one knee and proposed. His paramour enthusiastically said yes.

Come the day of the wedding, the groom, waiting for his future wife to arrive at the church, had a word with the church organist.

He asked if it was possible to break with tradition so that when the bride walked down the aisle, instead of the standard wedding march, the organist would play their song, the theme from *Robin Hood*. The organist, a stickler for convention, asked the groom if he was sure. The groom said he'd never been more sure of anything.

Minutes later, the bride's car pulled up outside. An expectant hush fell over the packed church, and as the doors opened, the organist struck up the *Robin Hood* theme as arranged.

The only problem was that the doddery old organist had never heard of Bryan Adams. So instead, he accompanied the blushing bride's ladylike procession with the jaunty and highly inappropriate 'Robin Hood, Robin Hood, riding through the glen' theme, from the hit sixties TV series of the same name.

golf *war*

A bloke at my mate's work is a keen golfer and frequently takes part in his club's charity days. He's pretty good but never wins because there's one fellow there who takes his sport very seriously and is virtually a scratch player.

On one of these competition days, the tasty golfer turned up as usual and was the first to tee off. But to the surprise of the other players, he completely fluffed his drive, fizzing it off into some bushes. Though he managed to recover on that hole, the pattern was set. When he fluffed his third tee shot in a row, hooking it out of bounds, the other competitors began to fancy their chances for real. 'He's playing like a right shanker,' muttered one.

After a dreadful nine holes out, the bloke spent a short while psyching himself up and mumbling that he couldn't possibly play as badly on the inward nine. But he was wrong. His tenth tee shot scudded along the deck, hit a bump and sailed through the air, landing just in front of a huge lake. The whole clubhouse gathered to watch what their top player would do next.

Alarmingly, the now rattled bloke completely sliced it and the ball plopped into the pond like a fishing line. A collective gasp emanated from the clubhouse as the golfer put his iron away, swung his golf bag round his head in rage and launched it into the water hazard as far as he could throw it. Then he marched, fuming, past the clubhouse,

throwing his glove into a tree as he strode back towards his car.

There was a stunned silence, followed by another audible gasp as the demoralised golfer came storming past the nineteenth again in a total strop. 'I'm having a very bad day,' he growled to the nearest contestant, and headed back at speed towards the water. Some people began to fear he might mean to do himself serious harm. After all, golf was his life.

The tension mounted as the golfer reached the lake and carried on walking until he was up to his thighs in the water. There he stopped, felt around under the surface and yanked up the water-logged golf bag he'd discarded. Then he ripped open a pocket and pulled out, to the mute amusement of all present, the dripping keys to his car.

going, going, *totally gone* . . .

Most airports have auctions every now and then to get rid of items from the unclaimed baggage department which are occupying valuable space. One bloke I know always goes down there and bids for the wallets.

He reckons he's going to get lucky and find one the Aga Khan's lost or something. But strangely people seem invariably to lose their wallets when they are empty, because there's never a sign of any cash when my mate gets hold of them.

Another regular down at these scavenging sessions, er, auctions, a young housewife, spotted a bargain she couldn't overlook and snapped up half a dozen packets of a popular proprietary washing powder.

Pleased with her haul at first, she soon complained to the manufacturers when her washing not only failed the window tests, but – contrary to the folklore of TV advertising – she would have happily swapped two packets of her new powder for one of her old brand that Danny Baker had nicked off her.

It was rubbish. It didn't shift stains in the slightest and the residue of deep-down, ground-in dirt meant her whites weren't bright whites anymore.

The puzzled company sent a sample away for analysis and discovered the reason for her wash-day blues. The woman had purchased six 30 kg boxes of pure heroin, and at a very good price too.

dead *cert*

A young friend was overjoyed to receive one of those spooky American baby dolls for Christmas. The life-like replica even came with its own birth certificate, much like the Cabbage Patch dolls you used to get a few years back. The little girl loved her cuddly baby doll and the two became inseparable.

The little girl played house with the plastic baby substitute, pushing it around in a pram. She gave it tea and even did the washing and ironing with the doll. She made believe with this politically incorrect conditioning toy until the sad worn-out plaything literally fell to pieces.

The poor angel was heartbroken at her favourite toy's demise. But nowhere near as distraught as the day she opened a letter addressed to her and found inside a death certificate, sent from the manufacturer.

a queer *reason*

An Antipodean chum works in the visa department of the Australian Embassy and was surprised when an old cockney character, at least 80 years young, tottered into the office asking for the necessary paperwork to emigrate.

The desk clerk gently proffered the observation that the chap was way over the normal age limit and asked him why he was so keen to start a new life down under.

'Is it to be with your family?' he enquired.

'No,' replied the old cove. 'They all live in Essex.'

'Health reasons then?'

'Nope. Fit as a fiddle that's never been played.'

247

'Then perhaps you could tell me why you're so keen to leave the country,' retorted the paper shuffler.

'Well, it's them new homosexuality laws,' the old codger grumbled. 'It used to be illegal under 21, then they legalised it for 18-year-olds – I want to get out before they make it compulsory.'

left *baggage*

One evening a Norwegian friend of someone at the squash club was driving with his wife from one end of the main north–south motorway to the other.

As anyone who's been to the land of the fjords will tell you, the country may not be very wide but it is very long, so deep into the night he was still driving.

Bored and tired, he resolved to have a pit-stop, recharge the batteries and empty his bladder at one of the many service stations. This he did, leaving his slumbering spouse in the passenger seat.

Suitably refreshed and relieved, he got back into the car, tuned the radio into a station that was playing some nice toe-tapping mellow music and roared away.

It was some hundred miles later that he realised things were rather quiet – then noticed to his consternation that his wife was no longer sitting in the passenger seat.

She'd obviously answered the call of nature back at the same service station; the problem was he was so weary, no matter how hard he tried, he couldn't for the life of him recall which service station he'd stopped at.

the Xmas *family break-in*

A nice family from Berwick, three sons in their twenties and a retired couple, planned to spend the Christmas holiday with in-laws at their new semi in Winchmore Hill, north London. They were due to arrive late on Xmas Eve, so the in-laws agreed to leave the side gate open and a back door key under a stone in the garden for them.

The family arrived even later than they thought, because the map the in-laws had sent them was useless. Exhausted, they finally came across the tree-lined road, followed the numbers and parked outside. One of the sons went to open the side gate, but it was locked, so he scrambled over the top. Then he unlocked the gate for the others, and they all stumbled about in the garden trying to find the stone and the key.

Then one of them hissed that the back door was open anyway, so they strolled in and collapsed in the lounge before unloading their stuff and making a pot of tea and sandwiches as quietly as possible. The mother, nosing around at her brother's new house, noticed some framed photos on the TV, but wasn't that surprised when she didn't recognise the people shown, even an old wedding shot of a couple she'd never seen before.

After their refreshments, the tired travellers crept upstairs, found empty rooms and went to bed. The next morning, Xmas Day, they all trooped downstairs for breakfast, and were confronted by two complete strangers sitting at the table. They had accidentally broken into the house next door.

shedding *a load*

A bloke from Bristol went to stay in the middle of the country with some old college friends who'd bought an ancient property and were 'doing it up'. Not being carrot-crunchers, the couple had rigged up some cooking facilities, but there was no electricity yet so they drove the ten miles for a take-away from the nearest curry boutique.

Swilling ale in the candlelight, the guest began to feel a pleasant state of inebriation coming on – as well as the call of nature he'd been dreading: the living room was full of masonry and dust, so God knows what the toilet would be like.

Eventually, he broached the subject, and the couple sniggered. 'It's a bit basic,' said the woman, biting her bottom lip nervously. Her partner explained the procedure. They didn't have a proper inside toilet, he explained, so he would have to find his way down the long garden to the shed, and do his business in there. 'Here,' he said, 'I should wear these if I were you.' And he handed his mate a pair of wellies, as well as some bum fodder.

Outside it was so dark you couldn't have seen one of Gyles Brandreth's sweaters if it was an inch from your face. The bloke didn't have a torch, so he had to feel his way tentatively across the boggy soil and fumble around for the outhouse. Eventually, his hands touched wood, and after a few seconds he was able to locate the door. On stepping inside, he had something of a surprise. The floor was very squelchy. 'Uh-oh,' thought the bloke, 'they haven't got round to fitting a pan yet, so they just use this as an earth toilet.' So he dropped his kecks, stooped down and relieved himself. Job done, he strode purposefully back towards the dim candlelight of the cottage.

Next morning, the bloke rose at the crack of dawn – either it was too quiet or some bird had aroused him (phwooaarr!) – and he decided he had to pay another visit to the shed.

By the cold light of day, from the outside it didn't look too bad. But inside was a real shock. Gleaming in the morning sun was an absolutely pristine avocado toilet and wash basin, all fully plumbed in, and not exactly set off by a rather nasty mess from the night before, slap bang in the middle of a new carpet.

house *of horrors*

A nice family moved into their new home, and had been saved the headache of redecorating by the previous owner. He was a dour man who'd offered the dwelling at a knock-down price because, he said, it was too big for him since his wife had left.

The only sour note was the putrid smell that seemed endemic. It was a real humdinger. After a few months, and despite the application of every type of proprietary disinfectant and bleach, as well as the dyno-rodding of the drainage system and plumbing, the stench still persisted, centred around the kitchen.

As it happened, a neighbour was standing in that very room at their cheese and wine housewarming party, held once the couple had settled in. She absentmindedly noted something odd. In her house next door there was an alcove in the wall, whereas the newcomers had a freshly wall-papered flat wall and shelving.

251

Without waiting for the party to clear, the host removed the shelves and broke through the plasterboard. There, in the old recess, was the reason for the festering odour: the remains of the previous owner's recently bumped-off wife.

Society

* The capacity at Wembley has to be reduced for rugby league finals, because the people in the crowd are that much fatter

* Hitler only had one ball. The Russians who found his charred body in the Berlin bunker carried out tests to see if they could use the evidence in propaganda

* It's quite common for dead passengers to travel around undisturbed for days on the Tokyo metro – even sometimes standing up

* The National Health Service only came into being because during the Second World War more than half the conscripts had rickets, polio or bad breath

* Dozens of commuters kill themselves on their way home every year by falling asleep. Apparently, they wake up confused and accidentally walk out of the train door between stations

* People who live near airports often have their greenhouses smashed by frozen sewage jettisoned from planes flying at 30,000 feet

* Shop mirrors are trick ones that make you look much slimmer

* Lord Kitchener was a notorious china thief, and society hostesses were alerted to his habit so they wouldn't kick up a stink when he lifted some porcelain

* During the war, Hitler flooded the south of England with thousands of fake £5 notes to destroy the British economy
* Don't bother separating clear bottles and coloured ones for recycling – they always mix them up again at the depot
* A headmaster who sent a sample of water from his school swimming pool for chemical analysis was surprised to receive the reply, 'This horse is very poorly and should be put down immediately.'

And finally, a few less-than-politically correct old tabloid favourites:

* Humberside council insisted on political correctness for the annual Christmas pantomime, and changed the show's name to *Snow White and the Seven Vertically Challenged Persons*
* Black bin-bags and blackboards were banned by Brent council, and 'Baa Baa Black Sheep' was outlawed in Haringey junior schools, for being racist
* Islington council only gives housing and jobs to pregnant, black, Jewish, disabled lesbians

wan*ted*

As part of our mission to collate all the world's greatest urban myths, we invite readers who would like to share their best stories with us to write them down and kindly send them to:

Phil Healey and Rick Glanvill
4 Driffield Road
Bow
London E3 5NF